ON A CLEAR DAY

ON A CLEAR DAY

DAVID BLUNKETT

with Alex MacCormick

Michael O'Mara Books Limited

First published in Great Britain in 1995 by
Michael O'Mara Books Limited
9 Lion Yard
Tremadoc Road
London SW4 7NQ

*A CIP catalogue record for this book is available from
the British Library*

ISBN 1-85479-684-4

1 3 5 7 9 10 8 6 4 2

Designed by Mick Keates

Phototypeset by Keystroke, Jacaranda Lodge,
Wolverhampton
Printed and bound in Great Britain by
Cox and Wyman Ltd, Reading, Berkshire

This book is dedicated to Valda
and Trevor Waterfield, my longstanding
friends, who have helped me
understand that there is life outside
politics.

My thanks go to:

Alex MacCormick, without whom this
book would not have been written as
she produced the first crucial draft

To Valda Waterfield, who had the
difficult task of going through the
book with me page by page and
producing a final version which reflects
the true me

To Annie Reid, who had the task
of the final editing and getting the
book together

To my sons, Alastair, Hugh and
Andrew, for their tolerance at
weekends when
I worked on the text.

'On a Clear Day You Can See Forever'

Contents

INTRODUCTION

PEOPLE MAY ASK themselves what this book is all about. Is it an autobiography of a politician, is it about Blunkett the man, or is it about dogs? In fact, it is about all three.

It was suggested to me that I might write about guide dogs and a little about my own life. I had certainly rejected the idea of writing a political autobiography at this stage. I would rather ensure that Labour gets into government and write about my experiences when I reach an age when retirement offers the time and space to do justice to it.

I did, however, agree that with a little supportive help it might be possible to produce a book which people may find of interest. So here it is: a thumbnail sketch of my life so far, with a great deal about guide dogs and little bit about politics.

I find when I meet some people for the first time, after greeting my guide dog, they tentatively raise the question of my blindness. I do not mind this. It is perfectly natural that people should wish to ask questions about how much I can see, whether it is possible to perceive colours, whether I can imagine what people look like from their voices and whether it is possible to dream when dreams are essentially pictures. This book attempts to answer some of those questions. The simple truth is that very few blind people have no perception at all of light and dark. I fall into the category of those who can discern light, particularly bright light – for instance, sunshine streaming in through a window. However, there are times when I get it wrong. I have often crossed a room in the evening to switch off a light only to find that it was already off.

I do imagine, and imagination is often very useful in the sense that it can enable me to focus in, and to look and behave in a perfectly normal way. I use my hearing, touch and smell, and also what I can only describe as an overall perception (or sixth sense) to enable me to feel when someone or something is close to me – perhaps when I am in danger of walking into a lamp post. Everyone has these faculties but does not necessarily have to use them. For me they are crucial.

So far as dreams are concerned, I dream the reality which I experience when awake, i.e. the combination of touch, smell and perception all blend together to form my dreams. I 'see' people in as much as I see them in my waking life. As is the case with sighted people, who see each other very differently, I also 'see' people differently. What some people find attractive, others do not. It saddened me recently when I heard that a young blind man had asked the Princess of Wales if she would allow him to feel her face. We have to be what we are. We do not perceive people by the shape of their nose at our fingertips, but by their voice, their manner and their approach. I do not need to feel the top of someone's head to know how tall they are, as I was once asked to do when young. I can hear it from where their voice emanates. The notion that this is not the case is quite bizarre.

I count not being able to see as an inconvenience rather than a disability. For example, if I am trapped at a drinks party talking to someone who is boring the pants off me, I cannot excuse myself by saying I have just spotted someone on the other side of the room I wish to have a word with, as sighted people are able to do. I have to rely on someone else spotting my plight and coming to my rescue. I might occasionally open a can of baked beans instead of a can of peaches. Sometimes, to compensate for lack of sight, there is a danger that I talk too much in a situation where silence would be more appropriate, where a glance would say all that is necessary. These are minor drawbacks and, although there are of course other more serious and embarrassing hazards, as I recount later in the book, most can be overcome.

Occasionally people say to me — and they mean it kindly — 'I really do admire you, you do so well . . . for a blind man.' Those killing words at the end are a real indication that there is still much progress to be made. The whole point is, of course, that we should all be judged by what we do and how effective we are irrespective of any 'disability'. Blind or partially sighted people do not belong to a separate group; for good or ill, we are all individuals in our own right. Although some people who work with and for the blind continue to refer to the 'world of the blind', there is no such thing. There is only the world we all inhabit and, whether blind or not, we all have to come to terms with that.

One of my motives for writing this book is to try to change people's attitudes in order to make it a little easier for blind people to cope with the world and to deal with the realities we face in everyday life.

From time to time I am criticised for not being a spokesman for blind people, but it was not for this purpose that I was elected. What I can do, however, is to set an example and encourage others to understand that helping disabled people achieve true equality in practice is everybody's responsibility.

So it is that I come to tell the story of my life, my struggle to overcome hurdles, obstruction and, some-times, downright bigotry. While I have outlined only the bare bones of my political life in order to provide a background, I have also deliberately avoided high-lighting deeply private matters in my relationships. I have, therefore, touched on the years of my marriage, but have not raked over the details as I have no wish to cause hurt or embarrassment to Ruth and my sons. Politicians cannot claim privacy and protection from the voyeurism of the media on the one hand and then themselves expose intimate aspects of their lives on the other.

At this stage of my life and my career there is a whole life still to be lived – hopefully, as much, if not more than, my adult life thus far – still to be grasped, enjoyed and rejoiced in. This book is by way of an interim report, light-hearted enough not to take either myself or my politics so seriously that I cannot see that real life goes on around me. What Denis Healey calls a politician's 'hinterland' is crucial to getting things in perspective.

If my story so far helps to encourage young people with a disability and their parents to face the future with optimism, then I will have done some good. In explaining the role of guide dogs and the importance of independence, dignity and mobility, I hope to be able to assist others and the work of the Guide Dogs for the

Blind Association in bringing about that freedom which so many blind people have enjoyed, thanks to their four-legged friend.

In addition to those already mentioned who have helped generously in the preparation of this book, I would particularly like to thank the following: Peter Smith and his colleagues at the Guide Dogs for the Blind Association; my staff – Jean Marples in Sheffield, and Alison Bartlett, Sarah Young, Sophie Linden and Conor Ryan in London; William Wake of the Royal National College for the Blind in Hereford; Mrs Susan Smith of Preston for allowing me to quote from her letter about Lucy; Matthew Vanes and the GDBA magazine, *Forward*, for allowing me to quote from his account of the vicissitudes of being a puppy walker's son; David Roberts, tape transcriber Elise Dillsworth and their colleagues at Michael O'Mara Books.

1

The Child is Father to the Man

To be honest it could not have been worse. As if it were yesterday I remember passing the cathedral with my parents as we made our way through Sheffield city centre. The warmth of the late afternoon sun that Sunday in September was beginning to fade. The cathedral bell was tolling for the evening service. Everything felt as though it were happening in slow motion, such was the tension as we bustled along hand in hand, Dad on my right, Mum on my left, to find the bus to Manchester Road.

We alighted at a strange place, somewhere I had never been before, and walked up a driveway with the scent of newly mown grass in the air. I shivered as we entered the coolness of what then seemed to me an enormous building. A peck on the cheek, 'Goodbye, son', and then they were gone.

All I had ever known before was my home and garden, and a bit of the immediate neighbourhood. Now, for the first time, I was alone in alien surroundings, cast adrift, abandoned. The anguish I felt was heart-wrenching as I stood bewildered, fighting back the tears, in the assembly hall of Manchester Road School for the Blind. It was a boarding school. I was four years old.

*

My mother, Doris Matilda Elizabeth Williams, was born in Leicester in 1903, one of four children. As a child she moved with her parents to Sheffield, where in her early twenties she married and had a child. When the marriage ended very unhappily in divorce in the 1930s, she set up home with her young daughter, Doreen, and her by then widowed father, Grandad Williams. She worked in factories of various kinds, including Stanley Tools, where high-quality hand-tools were made until the outbreak of the Second World War, when production was transferred to munitions. She then had the tricky task of spraying tracer bullets.

My father, Arthur Blunkett, was born in 1892 in Egham, Surrey, where his father was an agricultural labourer, but was brought up with his five brothers and sisters in the small Lincolnshire village of Wainfleet All Saints. There his parents are buried just outside the town in the graveyard of St Mary's Church, which to this day is lit and heated solely by Calor gas. As a youth he ran away to sea, sailing on a fishing smack out of Grimsby a phase of his life that left him with a lasting passion for geography if not much enthusiasm for life at sea. When at last he gave up seafaring, he did a spell as a waiter before finally settling in Sheffield around the time of the First World War. For reasons unknown, he was not called up to serve in the trenches abroad – presumably his was a reserved occupation. In any event, for the rest of his life he worked for East Midlands Gas Board, as it then was. By his first wife he had seven children, but such were the hardships of life in a two-up, two-down back-to-back house in the slums near Sheffield Wednesday football ground that only four of the children survived into adulthood and he had been left a widower.

My parents met in Sheffield and married in 1946 without much fanfare owing to the postwar austerity of food and clothes rationing. With Doreen and my mother's seventy-six-year-old father, James Henry Williams, they set up home in a two-bedroom council house in Everingham Road, in the Longley district of the city.

My father was very tall and upright, straight as a die – traits he seems to have inherited from his rather formidable mother. For a man then in his mid-fifties he was fit and surprisingly athletic with a fine head of bushy grey hair.

Despite having worked in factories, my mother believed in behaving in a ladylike manner. She was not a snob – far from it. She simply felt that everyone should try to 'put their best foot forward' and make the most of themselves. She was therefore always tidily turned out, though never fashionably dressed because she did not have the means. Friends said she had been pretty in her younger days and, despite considerable hardship and illness, she remained good-looking in her later years. She was fairly short and a little on the plump side – cuddly, I thought – which was the norm then given the nature of the food and lifestyle. Being slim was not something people tended to worry about in those days. What was of most concern was staying healthy and warm.

I was born in Jessop Hospital on 6 June 1947, when Mum was forty-three. It was by all accounts a difficult birth, made worse by the fact that she was suffering from a prolapsed uterus. In the council house, which was so cramped there was barely room to swing a cat, our arrival home from hospital was anxiously awaited by my father, grandfather and half-sister Doreen. When it was confirmed that her new baby was blind, it is said that my mother's hair turned white overnight. Fortunately, once she recovered from the shock and in the course of time her hair returned to its original colour.

When I was very young, there was hope that I could see a bit and glasses were prescribed. It is difficult to tell whether or not my sight diminished, although I do recall being able to discern the large headline of a *Hotspur* comic. I feel in my bones that I must have been able to see more than I can today. Nowadays only strongly contrasted light and dark are discernible. As the doctors eventually explained to my parents, the optic nerve behind each eye had failed to develop properly owing to the fact that my mother's and father's genes were not compatible – a one in a million failure. As a consequence, other parts associated with the optic nerves were unused and therefore gradually withered away. In 1947 there was no operation or transplant which could recreate the extremely fine network of nerves behind each eye, a particularly delicate area of the body, and even today with intricate micro-surgery there is little that can be done for a baby born with a similar problem. In any event, this is an area I prefer not to dwell upon. The best thing to do, the family decided, was to get on with life. Indeed, so well did my family succeed in this aim that I did not realise I was blind until I went to school, and even then the implications only gradually sank in.

Not long after my birth, twenty-year-old Doreen, who worked as a book-keeper, married and left home. Although she came back to see us quite often, Mum in particular missed her, not least because she had been an enormous help looking after Grandad. Most likely he missed Doreen too, but Grandad, a kindly, extremely strict and rather grumpy old man, was not inclined to show it. He was very traditional, old-fashioned even. His greatest bugbear was television, which he considered to be 'new-fangled' and refused to have in the house. So, we did not have a TV set until after he died. He also had heated arguments with my father about listening to the radio or 'the wireless', especially when my father scanned the short-wave band to tune into items of interest in other parts of the world. Nevertheless, Grandad was a genuinely caring man at heart, as witnessed by his devotion to his family and the support he gave my mother in the difficult time following the break-up of her first marriage. In return my mother looked after Grandad for the last twenty or so years of his life.

Grandad was too old and frail to play energetic games with a small boy, but he used to read to me, occasionally a children's short story, but more often news items from the *Daily Herald*. That may not sound very exciting, but I enjoyed it, and his grasp of history from having lived through so much was fascinating. I listened avidly to his tales of how, in the twenties and thirties, he had literally 'got on his bike' to travel from place to place in search of work. Initially he had worked as a coach painter, a skill combining bodywork painting and sign-writing; it was all done by hand then – no spray painting in his youth. His father had been born in the Newtown area in mid-Wales, he himself in Wolverhampton, while my mother was born in Leicester, so all in all he had seen a lot of the country before ending up in Sheffield. From listening to him I picked up much of my political awareness and developed an early interest in the wider world.

My mother also frequently read short stories to me: Enid Blyton books and other children's stories, as well as snippets from the newspapers. It must have been very demanding for her trying to teach a blind child and it makes me wonder why too few modern-day parents show any interest in encouraging their children to make the most of their education and improve themselves. Like so many of her generation my mother had an excellent command of English and knowledge of books, despite not having had much formal schooling. One of my current concerns as a parent is to persuade my own three sons to sit down and read a book. This is always much easier to do on holiday when there is no television and they are not allowed to take computer games with them; if they are bored, I tell them to read a book and, when they do, they enjoy it.

My Dad, on the other hand, was not a committed reader apart from the daily paper, but he was a thoughtful person with a vast fund of general knowledge, which he passed on to me. On walks together or with me seated on his knee, he would quiz me: what is the capital of Peru or China? Whereabouts is it? The picture of the world he gave me in those days before television made an enormous impact; it opened another dimension, broadened my horizons. I am a traditionalist in terms of education. I want everyone to have sufficient basic knowledge to make informed judgements, and be aware of their history and the environment in which they live. I am often surprised that, in spite of the instant communication which exists today, so many young people, my own sons included, have little grasp of geography or history.

My father was one playmate I could always count on as a child, providing he was not at work, of course. He spent hours playing with me, hiding beneath the table and pretending to be afraid as I shot arrows tipped with rubber suction pads from my bow or machine-gunned him with ping-pong balls. My mother looked on, half-smiling, half-scolding, and admonished us firmly if things got out of hand.

Since at the time there were no appropriate day schools in our region for blind or partially sighted children, my parents were told they had no choice but to send me, aged four, to board on the far side of Sheffield at Manchester Road School for the Blind (now called Tapton Mount). There they were allowed to visit me, but not take me out, one Saturday per month, and I was permitted to go home for one week-end a month. Mum and Dad did not want me to go to boarding school, especially at such an early age, but they had no choice; it was that or nothing. This is why the Sunday evening they took me to school was such an agonising one for all of us.

It would have been better if parents had been allowed to stay for at least part of the day to help their child get to know where he was going to sleep and to find his way round a little. Forty years ago the school authorities simply issued instructions, with the best of intentions no doubt, that parents should bring their child to the assembly hall, bid a quick farewell and leave him to it – they must not linger. Obviously this has a profound effect on an infant, who feels totally abandoned and terrified, particularly when he cannot see who or what is around him. It was one of the worst experiences of my life, as indeed it was for my parents. Mum told me years later how awful it was for them having to leave me; they had been racked by guilt and worry. In fact, contrary to instructions, they had stayed for quite a

while at a distance in the school grounds in the hope
that they might spot me.

In the meantime I was handed some uniform and
taken to a large dormitory which I was to share with
nine others. There I was shown my bed and the bedside
locker in which to store my personal belongings. Not
all the dormitories were as big; some were for six, but
these were reserved for older boarders. Sharing with so
many unknown small boys was frightening at first as
each one had his own quirks and habits, which one had
to learn. All the new boys were, like me, dreadfully
upset at leaving their parents; some wet their beds,
others cried themselves to sleep at night. Trying to
come to terms with one's own feelings at that age was
hard enough, let alone coping with the emotions of
the other boys. Also, as we soon discovered, we had
to do for ourselves all the everyday things our parents
usually helped us with – dressing and undressing,
washing, keeping track of possessions plus finding our
way round the dorm and the rooms beyond.

To help and look after us each dorm had a housemother, who was probably not much more than sixteen
or seventeen years old almost a child herself. She
too had to learn to cope with our emotional upsets by
giving us a bit of care and affection. How precious were
the swift hug and goodnight kiss bestowed nightly on
each of us as she tucked us up in bed – one of the few
signs of affection we received at school. I desperately
missed the hugging and affection of home, as did most
of my companions, and there was no real substitute.
Even the pets we were allowed to have later on could
not fill the gap. This deprivation had a lasting effect
on me well into adult life. Although my own sons are
now growing up fast, I often give them a hug, chiefly

because I believe it is important for them to feel that somebody cares about them, that there is security and stability, and that they are wanted and needed. My own parents made me feel all these things when I was at home, but there were great tracts of time away at boarding school when I felt desperately insecure and unloved. After a while one develops a protective shell, and it becomes hard to define and express one's emotions to others – at least that is how it was for me.

There were five or six housemothers in all, each of whom had charge of eight to ten children. They supervised us doing the minor daily tasks of brushing our teeth, bathing and drying. The large communal baths were situated in the basement of the old building and were approached by staircases and long corridors with bare plaster walls and uncarpeted floors smelling of dampness. Fortunately the bathroom area itself was warmed a little by an open coal fire, in front of which we had to dry our hair. Our housemother kept a close eye on us to ensure we washed behind our ears, did not topple over the fireguard into the fire and were thoroughly dry before we ran back to our dorm up the cold passages and stairs in our pyjamas and dressing-gowns.

Because the trip to and from the baths was slightly spooky, we small boys naturally invented tales about ghosts, ghouls and goblins lying in wait, in order to frighten each other. One or two members of staff even encouraged us to believe these fantasies with the aim of speeding us on our way. On bath nights, by the time we clambered into bed, we would be in such a state of nervous excitement that we would chatter away for hours despite constant admonitions to be quiet and go to sleep.

When at last the dorm fell silent, it did not necessarily mean we had gone to the Land of Nod, but merely that we were reading under the bedclothes. Once we had learned braille, it was only too easy to deceive our housemother when she popped her head round the door to check on us. Three or four years later most of us divided our time between reading and pressing our ears to portable radios to listen to the latest pop songs on Radio Luxembourg or to the next thrilling instalment of *Journey into Space*, which set our imaginations racing.

Another factor which lessened my unhappiness at Manchester Road was the camaraderie associated with learning to play cricket and football, which was great fun for an only child, especially as most of the others did not have an advantage over me. Since only one or two could see much, we played on equal terms. The football contained ball-bearings and the cricket balls had bells inside so that we could keep track of them. The fact that we were not capable of clever headers or tricky shots was neither here nor there. For us what counted was that at least fifty per cent of the time we connected with the ball rather than thin air or someone's shins and were getting plenty of exercise outdoors. At junior school I marginally preferred cricket to football. It was harder to hear the football, let alone locate the goals, on a large open pitch, whereas cricket was played closer to the school building, which made it easier to hear the ball. Cricket was, though, more dangerous. If a fielder got too close to the batsman, there was a fair chance of being knocked unconscious or of having his jaw broken as the batsman took his swing. I remember one lad caught a ball on his glasses and had to have an eye removed.

It may seem surprising that we were allowed to play such rumbustious games, but boys will be boys whether sighted or not. Wisely the adults in charge felt it was beneficial in developing confidence, bravery and self-reliance. This certainly applied to our three favourite pastimes: riding our bikes, go-karting and sledging.

Aged seven or so, learning to balance on a two-wheel bike was quite a challenge. More demanding was learning the best route to avoid falling head over heels every time the wheel hit a bump and, perhaps more vitally, how to take a sharp corner. If we took the corner too fast on the wrong line at the bottom of the grass slope by the school buildings, the bike would run into a low brick wall and we would go flying over the handlebars into the sandpit. In later years, I came to regard this as a robust but useful metaphor for life in general.

We constructed our own rather rickety wooden go-karts which consisted of a couple of flat planks to sit on with a pram wheel at each corner. The front wheels were on a wooden axle. We steered by pulling a length of string attached to the crossbar beside each wheel – very rough and ready, and sometimes the string broke while in mid-run. As we raced downhill, we aimed to swing the go-kart round at the last minute, before it hit the wall beneath the headmaster's study window. Quite often avoiding action was taken too late.

Much the same applied to sledging in winter. When covered with snow, the slope down to the school was irresistible. Sledging is risky enough at the best of times, but when neither you nor your sledging partner can see where you are going, it was quite a hairy experience, which added to the thrills, but also to the spills. The odds were 10–1 we would hit something or run slightly off-course into a snowdrift or a brick wall. It was all part of the fun, although I suffered many more cuts, bruises, broken fingers and fractured collar bones than the average, sighted kid. Looking back, I suppose it helped toughen us up.

At first, having been virtually an only child with few playmates my own age at home, being surrounded at school twenty-four hours a day by so many boys made me feel crowded out. Although that initial feeling gradually diminished, throughout almost sixteen years of sharing school or college dormitories I never came to terms with the lack of privacy. There was no quiet, private place to be alone or where one's belongings went unrifled. Privacy is therefore something I came to value greatly and although I have experienced desperate loneliness at times in my life, nowadays I never feel lonely when I am alone.

It may easily be imagined how excited I was when, at the age of five, I was first given a bedroom of my own at home. For some years my parents had asked the council to move us from Everingham Road, which was cramped, into somewhere larger. To begin with they were offered a smart, new house at the other side of the city, but Grandad, for reasons of his own, adamantly refused to go there. So instead we moved into an older property on the Parson Cross estate, on the industri- alised northern side of Sheffield, which had been built in the thirties. The house in Pollard Crescent contained three tiny bedrooms, a through lounge, a back porch off which was a coal bunker on one side and a lavatory on the other (which counted as an inside lavatory in those days) and – best of all – an upstairs bathroom with both bath and washbasin. These were previously unknown luxuries.

For the first few months, I shared my parents' bed-room, my cot pressed against one wall, while Grandad occupied the front bedroom. The third bedroom remained empty. Then, out of the blue or so it seemed, Mum and Dad came to a surprising decision. Despite being vehemently against getting into debt, they took out a hire-purchase agreement to buy me a proper bed, a wardrobe and a locker. I can clearly remember how delighted I was to have a room of my own.

While our new home seemed in many ways a palace compared with the old one, my abiding memory is of waking up on winter mornings and trying to wipe the ice from the inside of the windowpanes in my bedroom – fifties' version of double glazing! The house was freezing cold. I would rush to the bathroom to wash and then dress as quickly as possible before clattering downstairs to where Mum or Dad had lit a fire. But despite the fact that school was usually warmer than my room at home, I was always reluctant to return.

Life at Manchester Road School was not all fun and games; like small children everywhere, we had to learn to read and write. Having enjoyed being read to at home, I was longing to be able to read myself. In our case though it was an unusually slow, laborious process using braille writing frames. With a wooden-handled stylus we pricked dots through sheets of special paper on the same principle as braille, which could be read on the reverse by running one's fingertips over them. What took so long was that we had to write backwards, from right to left, in mirror image, so that when the paper was turned over the text could be read from left to right as usual. In order not to lose one's place on the large braille sheets, there was a cumbersome wooden frame which was moved down a notch at a time for each fresh line. The stylus had to be pressed hard through the thick paper, and the effort involved caused calluses on the fingers and palms of our small hands. It was all a difficult, frustrating discipline for us cack-handed, lively boys – but what joy it provided in the long run, once we had mastered it.

Later, when we were a few years older, we progressed to a Stainsby writing machine with six keys, which operated the stylus, plus a space bar. This was much faster and easier, but it was not until secondary school, around the age of thirteen, that I first experienced a much more modern piece of equipment, a Perkins Brailler from the United States. On this the keys when depressed forced the styluses upwards through the paper to create the dots on the face of the sheet. With this machine one could write from left to right and read the text while typing. Since then, of course, computerised braille software linked to braille embossers have become more commonplace, but I shall always have a soft spot for the braille writing frame (which I occasionally still use today) after those early struggles to master the back-to-front writing and doing it from right to left.

For arithmetic lessons we each had an indented wooden board into which metal pegs of various shapes denoting different numbers were slotted into appropriate holes. The chief hazard was that, if the frame were jolted or accidentally knocked over, all the tiny pegs flew out and we had to start again. Only rarely did we use an abacus. Not surprisingly, therefore, I preferred mental arithmetic, which was challenging and infinitely less fiddly. Geometry, trigonometry and algebra too came our way once we entered secondary school, and I still recall the fascination of leafing through the large braille book of logarithm tables.

Infected at an early age by my father's enthusiasm for geography, the school globe with its raised outlines of countries was an endless source of pleasure, giving a new dimension to the place names so often talked about during our 'quiz sessions'. History classes also led to my lifelong interest in the past, particularly the Industrial Revolution of the nineteenth century, and in early-twentieth-century political changes, which I eventually studied in greater depth at university. For some reason we were taught virtually nothing about medieval history – an omission later partly remedied, on a lighter level, by avid reading of the mystery novels by Ellis Peters, which feature the twelfth-century monk Brother Cadfael. Until I read her books I was largely unaware, for instance, of the early civil wars between Empress Maud/Matilda and King Stephen.

Nature studies and woodwork were also included on the timetable, and one particularly hair-raising woodwork class has left an indelible impression. One patient teacher, Wilf King, said to me, 'David, I'd like you to feel this piece of wood with a nail half in – then I'll show you how to hammer it in properly.' I did as he asked. Unfortunately he did not tell me to take my hand away fast enough so, instead of the nail, he hit my finger. It fractured, of course, and remains bent to this day. Nevertheless, my memories of woodwork classes are happy ones, boosted by my parents' unstinting praise for the misshapen creations I triumphantly took home: a stool too wobbly to sit on and an egg rack too unstable to risk holding eggs.

The coronation of Queen Elizabeth II took place during term-time when I was six years old. As part of the celebrations, a marquee was erected on the lawn. Although Coronation Day itself was rather damp, I

remember the following day being gloriously warm –
the smell of grass turning into hay remains with me.
'Land of Hope and Glory' was broadcast on a makeshift
public address system. There were lucky dips, into
which we all plunged for prizes, and lots of other stalls.
I remember upsetting a girl who was wearing a red
pinny (don't ask me how I know she had a red pinny!)
when I spilled lemonade down her front. While she
cried, I tried to console her. The day grew hotter
and hotter as the humidity rose and the sound inside
the marquee became deafening. I remember being
fascinated by reports of the enormous weight of the
State Crown and loved hearing on the radio the
constant patter of horses' hooves in the Coronation
procession.

Of the teachers I can only recall a few by name,
probably because they were notably kind or encouraging: Miss Lamb, who was a general teacher; Mr Gilbert,
who attempted to foster an interest in music; and the
head, Freddy Tooze, and his wife, Doris. Mr Tooze
eventually retired from teaching to work as an adviser to
the Government of Malawi. There he came to know
well Dr Hastings Banda, who, until he was ousted by
a general election in May 1994, was the longstanding
dictator and president of the country. Despite an almost
unequalled record for brutality and authoritarianism,
Banda nonetheless professed an interest in the education
of blind children, a concern not widely shared by other
leaders at the time.

Mrs Tooze, a genial and hearty woman, taught
us physical education, which was yet another risky
business, involving as it does vaulting over boxes and
horses, climbing wall bars and swinging on ropes. Most
of my class liked PE and hurled themselves around

enthusiastically, but I was not enamoured. I am not sure why. After all I was robust enough in cricket, falling off bikes, tobogganing and even breaking teeth trying to scale rocks in the Derbyshire Peak District. My dislike may have arisen from the fact that I was never any good at shinning up and down ropes. I did not mind the challenge of jumping over a box or horse once or twice but, at that time, I just did not see the point of repeating the exercise endlessly week after week. Now I would welcome such an opportunity of keeping fit. I also disliked, as I am sure everyone else did who came into contact with them, those spiky bristle floormats designed to protect us from harm but most lethal in terms of bare skin.

Apart from the desire to escape PE lessons and to see my parents, another reason I eagerly looked forward to going home for the once-monthly weekend or for the holidays was to spend time with my pets. At any one time there was quite a menagerie: rabbits, one or more white mice, a tortoise, a budgerigar and some goldfish.

Of the series of white mice I owned, two in particular come to mind. One was a female, or so I thought, who suddenly became rotund. Not knowing a great deal about such matters at the time, I became convinced she was pregnant. Then, even more suddenly, she died. With immense obstinacy I insisted on getting the vet to perform an autopsy. It transpired that she had died of an abscess, but vet pointed out consolingly that at eighteen months old she had lived to a fair age for a mouse. Considering she had been kept in a cage lined with cotton wool, particles of which must have floated everywhere for her to breathe in or eat, it was perhaps remarkable that she had survived so long.

My very favourite mouse though was Peterkin, for

whom my father constructed a special cage of wood with breathing holes in the roof and a glass panel at the front. I never knew why he used glass instead of the usual wire mesh, but the panel slid open easily for access and it gave Peterkin a window on the world, and my family and friends a view of him in his cosy home. At first I begged to have Peterkin's cage in my bedroom, but Mum put her foot down and so, astonishingly in the light of modern hygiene, he lived in the kitchen instead. There, every morning before he left for work at 4.30AM, Dad would feed him titbits for breakfast.

We also had a series of budgerigars, but the star of them all was Bimbo. Despite the name, the budgie was not a young temptress but a male named after a popular ditty of the day, the refrain of which was 'Bimbo, Bimbo, why are you on your owneo?' Nevertheless, he was not the most macho of birds and was easily driven to hysteria by my grandfather. Whenever Bimbo was let out of his cage and was foolish enough to land on Grandad's shoulder or his chair, Grandad would shoo him away by vigorously waving his beret under the bird's beak. With a high-pitched squawk Bimbo would flap off in a panic. One day, whether by accident or design we never knew, he dived into the rectangular goldfish tank. Evidently he discovered he liked it because thereafter, whenever he was let out, Bimbo would fly straight for the tank, jump in at one end, flap his way through the water to the other end and then leap out rather like a miniature seaplane. Behind him he left a trail of bewildered goldfish gazing upwards through the rippling surface at Bimbo's fast-disappearing tail feathers, wondering what on earth had hit them. In the meantime, Bimbo, looking mightily

chuffed, would perch somewhere to preen himself, all
the while muttering defiantly, 'Bimbo, Bimbo.'

Another clear memory is how one day, when I was
still quite young, seven baby rabbits sprang out of their
hutch while I was feeding them. Of course I had no
idea where they had gone, but I knew there was a
chicken-wire fence round part of the garden in which
we would sometimes let them have free run. On hands
and knees I scrabbled around trying to catch them, but
without success – they simply hopped out of reach.
Eventually my shouts of frustration brought Mum and
Grandad out to help, but it took a lot of huffing and
puffing to recapture them, particularly on Grandad's
part, as he tried not to curse out loud. My mother
disapproved of swearing even under such trying
circumstances as these.

Most of the time, while I was away at school, the
rabbits had to be looked after by my long-suffering
mother, but at the ripe old age of ten, Mr Tooze
allowed pupils to keep a pet at school. Since Peterkin
was no more, I chose one of the rabbits. Having been
sternly warned by both parents and teachers precisely
what the consequences might be for my pet should I
fail to care for him properly, I remember waking up
literally drenched in sweat one night in the dorm
having suddenly realised that I had not fed my rabbit
the day before. That feeling of acute guilt and dread
remains vivid. I never made the same mistake again.

In an attempt to assuage the feelings of homesick-
ness of the younger boys or perhaps to moderate the
ruffianly instincts of the older ones, the school also kept
its own communal rabbit, which each older pupil in
turn was meant to look after for a day. It lived with the
other pets in an area surrounded by an impenetrable

mesh fence in case wily rabbits, guinea pigs or hamsters escaped from their hutches or our clutches. I dearly loved my own pet, but felt extraordinarily sorry for the school rabbit, which seemed to me to get a raw deal since I was never sure anybody adult took overall responsibility for it. So, gradually, I took it upon myself to keep an eye on it, to be responsible for its welfare in much the same way as, over the years, I have tried to assume responsibility for things and people even if they did not want me to. This sense of obligation eventually led me into politics, but as a boy of ten or so this urge was largely focused on the school rabbit. Actually the creature was admirably resourceful, digging a burrow well out of reach of small boys poking at it or wanting to touch it, and it seemed to survive happily on the few leaves and morsels thrown to it. Indeed, it was precisely the sort of rabbit the school wanted us to be as children: tough, resilient and able to cope with life.

2

FAMILY SECRETS

'ALL HAPPY FAMILIES resemble one another; every unhappy family is unhappy in its own way' wrote Leo Tolstoy in the memorable opening to his novel *Anna Karenina*, while, equally astutely, Alan Bennett in *Kafka's Dick* observes that, 'Every family has a secret, and the secret is that it's not like other families'. As a boy protected from and ignorant of the hardships of my parents' early lives, I probably thought of my relations more in terms of *My Family and Other Animals*, had I known at the time of Gerald Durrell's hilarious memoirs of his family. Certain members of a family always seem to stand out because they are slightly more interesting or eccentric than the rest – and this was the case with my relations.

At home in Sheffield with Mum, Dad and Grandad Williams, for most of my childhood I felt like (and in practice was) an only child. Gradually, however, it dawned on me that I was but a sprig on a fairly substantial family tree.

Although, as I have already mentioned, Grandad could be grumpy and we had our differences, he and I enjoyed having each other around. But caring for him became an increasing burden for my mother as he grew older and was less able to help himself. What she found most difficult was the fact that this responsibility was not shared by her siblings, who knew how ill she had become. No one said, 'Father, come and spend a fortnight or so with us, and give Doris a break.'

To be fair, my mother's sister Mary, who at the time of writing is in her late seventies, has always suffered from mental health problems and so would never have been a suitable carer. But it was a different matter with my two maternal uncles, Eric and Joe, towards whom my mother showed no resentment. They did not actually refuse to help. They simply never offered. Eric and Joe regarded it as the daughter's job to look after their father – 'women's work'. All too frequently this attitude still prevails, which is why nearly all the six million carers in Great Britain today are women – the unsung heroines of the Welfare State without whom our society would be sunk.

Joe and Eric, both of whom lived in Sheffield, had served seven-year trade apprenticeships and were skilled craftsmen in machine-tool engineering works. Eric, I believe, had design skills and had a slightly better job than Joe. Much of their leisure time was spent fishing. At one point Uncle Eric even produced his own specially designed fishing reel, but was unable to get it into commercial production owing to opposition from the cartel of existing fishing-tackle manufacturers, who did not want competition. For the rest of his life he harboured considerable feelings of resentment at being thus thwarted. Uncle Joe, meanwhile, concentrated his efforts on becoming a crown green bowls champion.

The Blunkett side of the family was both more numerous and, to a child at least, rather more intriguing. My grandfather, Sanders Blunkett, died at the age of sixty-seven, before I was born, but I can clearly recall being somewhat intimidated by Grandma Blunkett. A frail but very dignified old lady in her eighties when I was a small boy, she spent her life propped up in bed at her home in Wainfleet, Lincolnshire, about five miles from the east-coast resort of Skegness.

So it was that every summer, during the school holidays, we would stay for two weeks in a boarding house in Skegness. It was our treat of the year, for which Dad saved every penny; after marrying my mother, he did not go out to pubs or working men's clubs. In fact, he rarely drank, but one of his pleasures was his pipe tobacco or his 'smokes', as he called it. As Dad worked for the Gas Board and not in the steel industry, there was no need for us to take our holiday during Sheffield's 'Works Weeks' at the end of July and early August, although in fact that is when we often chose to go. 'Works Weeks' – also known as 'Wakes Weeks' in other parts of the north – were traditionally the period when the engineering and steel plants closed down for maintenance. The practice has now largely died out owing to modern, twenty-four-hour, seven-day-week continuous working. Grandad, never very keen on varying his routine, preferred to stay at home.

From our temporary seaside base, we would make the annual pilgrimage to our relations in the area. The distances seemed enormous as the local bus, which often ran only once a day in each direction, bounced its way along narrow, winding back roads between Skegness, Boston, Wainfleet and wherever. It was quite an adventure as the bus lurched unsteadily with its passengers through unknown territory.

With Grandma Blunkett lived her daughter Olive

and Aunt Olive's husband Cyril. To an ever-hungry small boy Uncle Cyril seemed to have the perfect job: he worked in a bakery and ran a delivery round through the back lanes of Lincolnshire, carrying not only fresh bread, buns and cakes but also other entirely unrelated items requested by isolated countryfolk; sometimes he even collected people's pensions for them. But it was, of course, the cakes and buns which most interested me, and not a few of them came my way via Aunt Olive, a motherly character with no children of her own who spoiled everybody, including me.

Aunt Nora, on the other hand, much more closely resembled Grandma and was an imposing, patrician figure. Despite the fact that she, her husband Arthur Dodsworth and their two children were poor, they behaved in a gentrified manner and carried themselves with great dignity.

An entirely different character and one of my favourites was cousin Muriel's father, Uncle Mick, who worked for many years as a painter and decorator for the local council. Mildly eccentric, warm and outgoing, he was at heart a frustrated farmer who lived in one of the very few early council houses in Wainfleet. Despite rules forbidding tenants to keep animals on council property, he nurtured a large pig in a homemade sty at the bottom of the garden as well as numerous bantams, which had free run and pecked round visitors' feet. Keeping a wary eye open in case the voracious pig tried to eat my hand, he would let me feed scraps to both the pig and the birds. I enjoyed hours searching out the little bantam eggs in the nooks and crannies where they had been secretly laid and collecting crab apples for jellymaking. For a town child, it was heaven.

From the village road Aunt May and Uncle Mick's home was approached by a small bridge across a ditch and a path up the front garden. As soon as the front door opened I could smell paraffin, which was used for heating and cooking because there was no electricity, and to this day that distinctive smell always reminds me of Uncle Mick's house and the fun I had.

Rather more aloof and disorganised was Uncle Tom, who ran a fish and chip shop in what seemed to be the middle of nowhere. A strange man, he would welcome us warmly upon our arrival, but funnily enough only ever offered us yesterday's cold, left-over chips to eat. And then there was Herbert or Uncle Nib, as he was always called. What his job was remains something of a mystery to me, but it is highly unlikely that he was a writer, despite the nickname. Having moved down south to live in Southampton, Uncle Nib would take a brief holiday each year to coincide with our stay in Skegness so that he could see Dad and catch up on family news. He too had an odd side.

One of the delights of the resort for young and old alike was the beach: lounging in deckchairs, building sandcastles, paddling or merely wandering about observing the doings of others. Uncle Nib, however, dressed to the nines in his carefully pressed Sunday suit and his best squeaky shoes, adamantly refused to set foot on the sands. It was not necessarily beneath his dignity to remove his shoes and socks; it was simply that he did not like sand and would never for a second contemplate walking barefoot on the hateful stuff. Equally he could not risk spoiling his squeaky shoes. Uncle Nib seemed oblivious to the fact that his foible might mar the day for the rest of us. My parents, on the other hand, ever mindful of the feelings of others

and 'doing the right thing', never tried to dissuade
him from his thoughtless attitude. As a consequence,
afternoons in the company of Uncle Nib were spent
miserably contemplating other families enjoying themselves on the beach while I remained bored at a safe
distance.

These uncles and aunts were not my parents' only
siblings. We tend to forget nowadays that for their
generation and socio-economic group infant mortality
was high. In one of my favourite novels, *Cider with
Rosie*, Laurie Lee echoes my parents' shaded memories
and half-spoken allusions to brothers, sisters and
children who had not lived long.

Naturally enough, busy uncles and aunts seldom had
time spare to play with a visiting nephew, so I relied
heavily on my parents and on Uncle Ron. Ron was one
of my half-brothers by my father, but I always called
him uncle because he was so much older than me. He
often joined us for a break in Skegness. My mother was
never comfortable with my father's surviving children
by his first wife, so we did not meet up very often, but
since his death, I have tried to keep in touch with his
family.

From our many stays in Skegness, there is one
episode which stands out in my memory with unusual
clarity. One grey, damp day my parents took me for
a stroll in the ornamental gardens surrounding the
boating lake. Feeling, as ever, sure of myself and full of
independence, I struck out ahead of them along the
path. What little vision I had at the time – as I said, I am
still convinced that as a child I could see more than I do
today – led me to believe I could discern the difference
in the visual texture between the tarmac path and the
lake. A heavy shower of rain had made any chance of

doing so — even if it were not purely imagination — quite impossible.

When my feet touched the bottom of the lake, it was as though I were on springs. So fast did I seem to soar from the water that I had the distinct impression the water had not touched me. Of course, I was mistaken. I was absolutely drenched and, more to the point, so too was my treasured braille watch, given to me by my parents for my last birthday. One of the things braille watches cannot be is waterproof. Both the rim of the lid over the face and its tiny hinges at the back enabled the water to seep in. I was very upset not only because the watch was my pride and joy but also because I knew how hard Mum and Dad had worked to scrape together the money to buy it. It was, therefore, an immense relief when, the following morning, I woke to find my watch ticking away merrily. All was well, although not for long. Forty-eight hours later it ground to a permanent standstill, having rusted inside. From then on I learned to be a little more cautious about the extent of my power of sight — a lesson I was to learn again in later life.

Our holidays in Skegness always seemed to pass too quickly. Then it was back once more to Sheffield where the daily routine was resumed. Dad returned to his gruelling shifts working for the Gas Board, while Mum took up her oft-repeated lament that, because of the appalling hours he worked, he never had enough free time to spend with us.

From time to time, when I was home from school and Dad had the weekend off, my mother would make a picnic and the three of us would escape the grimy industrial suburbs on a local bus to spend a day among the hills and dales of Derbyshire. Sandwiches finished,

Dad and I would wander off together, just the two of us, chatting all the while, he describing the scenery or any interesting sights or simply quizzing me to see if I was up to the mark on general knowledge. Dad helped me to be robust in terms of overcoming my 'disability' and not to regard myself as handicapped; he never treated me as a blind child, but as he had his older sons.

Occasionally we would walk from home across our council estate towards Ecclesfield and the Jewish Cemetery to the north, but whenever we did so Mum would berate Dad for allowing me to return footsore. More frequently, though, he and I would simply walk round Ward's Cemetery beside the railway line close to Sheffield Wednesday football ground. In retrospect I wonder what the morbid interest was in cemeteries. The Hillsborough stadium, where Dad sometimes took me to matches, was a Mecca. We would sit on the wall behind the goal – something no longer allowed for safety reasons – and shout ourselves hoarse. From the back garden of our house, the roar of the crowd could clearly be heard on match days. It was easy to discern from the sound whether our team had had a near miss or a goal scored against them. I have been a keen supporter of Sheffield Wednesday ever since and one of my favourite photographs is of me with the Rumbelow's (Coca Cola) Cup, taken when they won the Final in 1991.

Our prime time for talking, Dad and I, was while we were gardening. At the end of our garden there was an area of disused scrubland which belonged to the local council. In return for a minimal amount of extra rent, Dad was given permission to extend our garden by fencing in a plot to transform into an allotment. Since I was obviously unable to see any other vegetable patches, it had never occurred to me that such things existed in an industrial city and certainly not where you could grow crops good enough to eat.

To begin with Dad set me to work on a bare patch in the new allotment. There I worked off surplus energy digging furiously, soil flying in all directions, at a safe distance from him. Gradually, as I improved, I was allowed to approach the planted rows, although I still sometimes dug up the wrong things. He taught me to feel the difference between edible plants – our crop – and weeds, how to plant seeds and seedlings, and how to nurture them. At the end of a hard session digging, I would flop into bed happily exhausted and there proudly finger the calluses on my hands before at last falling sound asleep. As a busy politician, at the end of a seemingly endless day spent sitting in tedious meetings, I sometimes think of those far-off days when I used to go to sleep physically exhausted as opposed to being merely emotionally and mentally drained as I am now. A balance between the three would suit me much better.

Thinking of happy times with Dad leads to the reflection that, as far as I can recall, there was only one aspect of his character I would have wished to change. It was something both Mum and I found acutely embarrassing. Unlike my mother, whenever my father met someone he regarded as well educated, he would seek to impress that person by trying to mask his Yorkshire accent, trying to imitate the man or woman to whom he was speaking. It seemed an unnecessary pretence and I so wished he wouldn't do it. As a small boy I vowed I would never make the same mistake. Ironically my own accent has been subconsciously modified by years spent in Shropshire and elsewhere, but I would never purposely either put on a broader

Yorkshire accent when talking to constituents or tone
it down for southerners. I am proud of being a
Yorkshireman.

Mum looked after the flowers in the allotment, and
she also made delicious pickles with the fair variety of
vegetables that Dad and I brought home – my favourites
were cabbage, sprouts and root vegetables, particularly
beetroot. Whenever I helped her scrape carrots for the
next meal, we used to jest about them making me see in
the dark. I have warm recollections of my mother's own
version of Lancashire hotpot or Irish stew, which with
no lack of appreciation we called 'hash', superb fish
with potato scallops fried in batter, liver and bacon, her
Yorkshire puddings with jam, and my father's obsession,
steamed puddings. All these dishes, although prepared
on the gas cooker, were kept warm on what was known
as the 'back-to-back range', a black, cast-iron oven in
the kitchen heated by the fire in the front room. The
range did have a hob, but because it was not hot enough
for cooking, it was used solely for warming bricks
which were then wrapped in cloths for heating the
beds in winter – a kind of old-fashioned hot-water
bottle. On washdays, with the range pumping out
heat and with the exertion of pummelling the clothes
in the 'dolly tub', it was hot work for Mum – and
for me too, when I had the chance to help her. She
encouraged me to regard myself as the equal of any
other lad of my age, to think of what I wanted to
achieve instead of grumbling and dwelling on the worst
aspects of life.

Much has changed in such estate homes since then.
There were sounds which have now largely disappeared, but which as a boy of eleven or twelve I took
for granted as part of everyday life: the clattering and

dust as the coalman came to refill the coal bunker once a fortnight or so; the hopeful cry of the rag-and-bone man as his horse-drawn cart clip-clopped along the road; the call of the muffin man who sold crumpets; the chink of bottles as the milkman made his rounds; even sometimes the hissing of the itinerant knife-grinder's wheel. These and so many other events are virtually Dickensian to most modern children and yet they were common in the fifties and early sixties. And who would have guessed that the trams which rattled along the streets in my youth and were then summarily banished as out of date would reappear in modern form as part of Sheffield's new rapid transit system known as Supertram?

By the autumn of 1959 I was twelve years old and the minor dramas and excitement of the family holiday in Skegness had faded. By December I was totally pre-occupied with the dread prospect of moving away from Sheffield in the New Year to start secondary school at the Royal Normal College at Rowton Castle in Shropshire. This meant saying goodbye for ever to most of my classmates, who were going on to other schools for the blind in various parts of the country. At the time there was in the whole of England only one national grammar school for blind boys, Worcester College – akin to a public school – entrance to which depended upon passing a residential version of the nationwide eleven-plus examination, taken at the age of twelve. Without benefit of a visit or an interview, I was adjudged unsuitable and so had no option but to pursue my secondary education at the less intellectually demanding and socially aware boarding school at Rowton. Mr Tooze evidently seemed to feel this was the most appropriate school for me, as the following report by him reveals:

> The psychologist said he was a boy of undoubted average intelligence with a vocabulary associated with a higher intelligence quotient.
>
> David is a very co-operative, conscientious, hard-working boy. He takes a very serious attitude towards work which is shared by his parents. His standard of attainment is good for this school, and I am quite certain he is the right type of boy to succeed where hard work and application are required. His desire to make the best of himself is rather remarkable. He is certainly worth a trial at the Royal Normal College.
>
> He is a strong, well-built boy, well adjusted to his blindness, mobile and active.
>
> F Tooze

The maelstrom of emotions caused by this prospective change seemed to be the sole cloud on my horizon. Then, like a bolt from the blue, life at home too was irreparably shattered.

Dad had worked for the East Midlands Gas Board for forty-seven years, virtually all his adult life, and should have retired in 1957, when he reached the age of sixty-five. But the management asked him to stay on for an extra three years to train new recruits and to update the system. I suspect he decided to accept the offer because my parents needed the income. It would have been hard to raise a boy coming up to his teenage years, care for elderly Grandad and run a home on what was then a minimal occupational pension. Also Dad liked his work – it was an important part of his life.

He was a foreman at the gas works operating a procedure known as a water gas plant, which transformed coal into gas and, in the process, created coke. Well respected and well liked, I think today, in similar circumstances, he would have been promoted to a managerial post, since the manager himself used to ask Dad what was going on and how to do things. But, instead, he was still working long shifts in potentially dangerous conditions. In December 1959, owing to the incompetence of a fellow worker who had failed to repair a safety device as instructed, Dad fell into a giant vat of boiling water. He saved himself from total immersion by hanging on to the rim by one arm, but naturally the scalds to the rest of his body were horrendous. He died in the Royal Infirmary a month later, on 7 January 1960.

The fortnight after Dad's death was spent comforting my mother and remembering. Remembering the exact time, 3.34PM, when he had died; how I had visited him shortly after he had undergone plastic surgery and the terrible smell of burnt flesh, which remains with me today; and the astonishing fact that he had asked about my pet rabbits despite the wanderings of a mind swamped by anaesthetic and pain-killers. It was a dreadful, agonising end. At the time I felt tremendous hurt, anger and bewilderment at his unnecessary and painful death; in later years such feelings led to my involvement in the fight to improve regulations concerning health and safety in the workplace. But that January we were left totally bereft in more ways than one.

Following a mournful funeral attended by family and friends, Dad was buried in an unmarked grave in Burngreave Cemetery. A headstone was beyond our means; only many years later, when I was finally in full-time employment, could I at last afford to erect a headstone on his grave. My mother found herself in dire financial straits while for the best part of two years she battled to win compensation for the accident.

The Gas Board took a harsh stance, more reminiscent of the worst private employer than a publicly owned industry. The Board argued that compensation was intended to replace income which would have been earned during an employee's working life. Since my father was over sixty-five, he had had no working life left, they said, and therefore compensation was inappropriate. In the meantime it was discovered that Dad had fallen behind with payments on his union subscription. Such an oversight was not uncommon, for many members were erratic payers and, in any case, he had obviously not expected to have an accident. Eventually, after some argy-bargy, the union agreed to accept payment of his back dues from fellow workers and to fight the case in court on my mother's behalf.

In the end the court awarded a small amount to Mum and also a small sum to me. In a paternalistic way, the court's attitude at that time was that the compensation should be held in trust on my behalf by the court, rather than allowing my mother to deal with it as she saw fit.

As a result of all this protracted legal wrangling, until the meagre compensation was awarded, my mother was desperately poor. I do not use the term lightly. Those who have never experienced real poverty are all too often very sentimental about it and about poor people in general. I have to smile at this and think: if only you knew what it was like, you would know all about aspirations and expectations, and why it was that, in the community in which I grew up, escaping the poverty trap and achieving success were the key aims. That is why I am so keen to give people ladders out of poverty: to give them a hand up rather than a hand out. My mother, at one stage, only had bread and dripping in the house for us to eat. There is nothing even faintly romantic about being poor and hungry.

So it was at this point in my life, with my father dead and my mother struggling to manage and look after Grandad, that I left Sheffield for the unknown of the new boarding school.

3

Turning Point in the Marches

CEDARWOOD, YEW, DAMP vegetation, clear crisp air. I inhaled deeply, trying to disguise my nervousness and apprehension as I climbed from the car which had dropped me off at Rowton Castle.

The first term at a new school is never easy. At the start I felt a mixture of excitement, fear and loneliness, and had terrible collywobbles. Because of my father's death, I arrived late, three weeks after the beginning of the spring term, and everyone else had bagged beds, lockers and wardrobe space. Worse yet, they had already made friends, including the few pupils I already knew from primary school in Sheffield, some of whom had joined the previous September. Apart from me, only Christine Pine from Barnsley, a former classmate, had started after Christmas, but even she seemed well entrenched with a new circle of buddies. I had missed the early weeks of term crucial to blending, and late-comers are always regarded as outsiders.

There was another, in some ways equally tricky, hurdle to overcome: clothing. This was the era when boys of twelve or so gave up wearing shorts in favour of long trousers, but my mother was always a bit old-fashioned and in any case did not have the money to rig me out in new clothes. Thus I arrived at Rowton in short trousers, which attracted considerable mockery and caused me acute embarrassment. Nevertheless the experience toughened me up. Once my legs had been slapped a few times, I learned to look after myself and deliver a sharp retort. The oldest boys were sixteen, and a four-year age gap in a boarding school creates a big difference in height, weight and ability. I knew I had to learn rapidly to fend for myself. It was, in many respects, a useful preparation for a life in politics.

My new school was a Queen Anne building constructed between 1696 and 1704, which had then been transformed into a neo-Gothic castle at the beginning of the nineteenth century. The result is a cross between a country house and a Beau Geste fort. Of red stone quarried locally in Corvedale, the main façade is imposing with a tower on the left, a crenellated roofline, and on the right a gabled wing with two corner turrets. Fifty yards away a group of inoffensive modern red brick buildings provided dormitory accommodation and recreation rooms with boys and girls in separate blocks. In front of the castle still stands one of the largest and therefore oldest cedars of Lebanon in Europe; its girth was over eighteen feet, when I was there, and its lowest branches tipped the ground. In due course I would come to spend quite a lot of time beneath its boughs, its shade being always cool and calming.

On one side of the building a fortified archway gave on to a cobbled courtyard, while on the other, behind the prefabricated typing and commercial studies block, was an area of tarmac for football and roller skating. At the rear of the house a tall avenue of ancient limes receded towards the jagged outlines of the Welsh mountains not far distant.

Seven miles west of Shrewsbury along the road to Welshpool, Rowton was part of what was then known as the Royal Normal College for the Blind, later renamed the Royal National College. The name 'Normal' came from the French term *école normale* in deference to the fact that the further education branch of the College at Albrighton was to some extent a training ground for music teachers. The name was eventually changed because few people understood the derivation. Originally founded in 1872, the College was evacuated from Norwood, South London, during the Second World War. The Castle, known as the School Department, was a secondary school for twelve- to sixteen-year-olds; further education was provided at Albrighton Hall, known as the Training Department, some miles away to the north of Shrewsbury.

Even as a twelve-year-old I was fascinated by the history of the original Rowton Castle and by the Welsh Marches or borderlands. Offa's Dyke is a mere ten miles or so from here and the region is dotted with ancient forts, castles and abbeys – the *Strongholds and Sanctuaries* of Ellis Peters' book. My imagination was fired by the discovery that in medieval times Rowton had belonged to Sir Robert Purnell, Lord High Treasurer of England to King Edward I. It had also for many years been owned by the powerful Abbey of Shrewsbury, which possessed huge tracts of land all round the town until Henry VIII's dissolution of the monasteries. Much later, while he was briefly MP for Shrewsbury, the estate belonged to Benjamin Disraeli until, in 1880, the property was taken over by his political secretary.

It was natural, therefore, that one of my favourite subjects continued to be history, although I enjoyed geography, English and general studies too. Unfortunately we were insulated from developing an interest in science by the simple lack of any lessons. There was no hands-on practical biology, physics or chemistry, which I later regretted, but as at Manchester Road School the College authorities were obviously afraid that chemistry experiments would end in disaster. This assumption may well have been valid as we would almost certainly have found a way to blow the place to smithereens.

Funnily enough, the first occasion when I got into serious trouble was over explosives or, to be more precise, fireworks. Several days before Guy Fawkes Night I was in the grounds, happily messing around, letting off some fireworks bought on my last trip to Shrewsbury, when along came Rowton's Deputy Head, Elizabeth Chapman.

'What do you think you're doing, David?' she rasped.

'Letting off fireworks, Miss,' I replied, trying to sound as innocent as I could.

This was judged to be 'giving cheek', for which I was gated, that is banned from leaving the school grounds, and given detention which involved having to copy out dictionary entries for what seemed like hours on end. It was very dreary.

The school lay in fifteen acres of grounds, surrounded by the rolling countryside of Shropshire, an area which in the past had been well husbanded and clearly a source of considerable bounty. I am sure Shropshire has more than its fair share of nettles (presumably because it receives more than its fair share of rain!) and I remember distinctly the impact the smell of those nettles made in the heat of the summer as I would walk up the school driveway, often by myself, sometimes thinking, sometimes simply enjoying the birdsong and the sounds around me. Breathing in this heavy scent acted as both a warning to beware of straying from the driveway or earthen track and also a wonderful reminder of the bounty of summer.

Just before the end of the driveway was 'Jacob's Ladder', a tree whose branches conveniently enabled even the clumsiest to get at least part-way up its trunk. The problem when you cannot see is twofold: firstly, you can locate a branch quite easily when it is above your head, but, as you pull yourself up, you are quite likely to hit the one you didn't find; secondly, you have to remember fairly carefully the way you came up and which branch it was that you had tested for its strength and durability. Many of us came a cropper, although the number of branches which could no longer take our weight obviously diminished as accidents occurred!

It was this sense of adventure, as well as an undoubted desire to break the boredom of boarding school, which led to some of us engaging in nocturnal expeditions. Again, this was a summertime activity. There were enormous attractions to creeping out on a balmy June or July evening, but none too many in November or January. How often did members of staff looking out of their windows espy us making our way down the driveway through the yew hedge and into the dilapidated kitchen gardens? Only once or twice were we apprehended.

Climbing into the garden was no more of a challenge for us at night than it would have been, of course, during the day, but the hazards were just the same. Getting on top of the wall was one thing, but getting down the other side quite another. I distinctly remember the night when, egged on by fellow conspirators, I lowered myself gingerly from the wall only to find myself up to my knees in a water-filled butt. The little sight which some of those with me possessed did not appear to be all that useful by the light of the moon, although for some reason I do not remember any of them carrying a torch. Minor cuts and bruises were sustained on our expeditions, which included lashing together old barrels to make a very unstable raft for the overgrown pond, or discovering where we could gather berries and fruits.

It was in my first year at Rowton Castle that I put paid to my politician's permanent perfect smile when I broke a very substantial piece off one of my front teeth. By the time a dentist offered me a cap thirty years later, I had decided to live with it and not bother. It happened when a group of us decided to hold a jousting match. This involved knocking each other around with rolled-up braille magazines, which pack a considerable punch, while standing on unstable wooden chairs. The sight of youngsters who could not see knocking the hell out of each other with what amounted to foot-long truncheons, while precariously balancing on chairs, must be one to treasure! The consequences, however, could be dire as I discovered when I slipped and fell, breaking a tooth on the back of a chair. All such incidents obviously had to be reported to parents and, in my case, a promise of remedial action, which in the event never occurred.

End-of-term or annual reports often paint a distorted image of a child, emphasising not so much the charac-ter as the sharp edges of the individual youngster. Not surprisingly, after the trauma of my father's death, my early reports illustrated an uphill battle. My conduct left 'much to be desired. On occasions he can be a paragon of virtue. At other times, he is rude, noisy and downright disobedient.' Readers will be pleased to hear that things did improve as the years went on! As for physical education, I was 'fair but apt to grumble. Uses his energy in talking rather than in activity'. Comments like 'Shows off to gain attention' reflected the need to work on social skills, and the frequent 'Makes too much noise' clearly indicated that I was a politician in the making! Strange as it may seem, I think it was my being at boarding school which contributed to my being anti-social. The change from living on a quiet council estate compared with the spacious yet noisy and brash environment at school presented many obstacles. Rowdiness and a lack of finesse were, in my school, the order of the day.

In common with all parents with children at boarding school, my mother had to share responsibility for my upbringing with the school. Her letters, a few extracts of which are cited below, indicate very clearly her wish to ensure that her care for me did not mean giving me everything I wanted.

24 January 1960

Dear Miss Chapman

Thank you for your letter. I am pleased to know my son David seems to be settling down to his new life and surroundings. I expect it will take him a little while longer, having recently lost his father, for whom we both had a strong affection . . . Pardon my sending the doctor's note. In the year 1956 we had to seek the advice of an ear specialist. After which David had an operation for sinus trouble, the specialist then advised no swimming for the next two years. This time elapsed in August 1959. We allowed David to swim in the sea and I am pleased to say no ear trouble.

2 December 1966

. . . I am apprehensive of the ice-skating, if this being the object of their visit to Birmingham. However if other parents are agreeable to their sons taking the trip, I will also give my son permission . . .

21 July 1967

I would like you to know I appreciate all the instruction, the care and attention given to my son David during his life at the College. I am proud of his achievements. Thank you for your understanding when I have been in doubt . . .

In sharing with readers my mother's letters through my years away at school, I am revealing the deep love that she had for a young man who inevitably was beginning to grow away from her. Her gentle and old-fashioned style of writing reflected her dignity, but also her deference to the professionals who now had day-to-day charge of my upbringing. It is hard to exaggerate the impact that my mother's expectations had on my own efforts to improve myself. I cared deeply what she thought and how she felt about me. Whenever I was in trouble, it was not myself that I thought about or the punishment, but only what my mother would think and how hurt she would be. If there was a threat which mattered to me, it was that I would cause her distress and that in her eyes I had not lived up to her expectations. I was her son and, much later in life, I was to want her to be proud of me and to feel that I had not let her down.

Permission had to be sought for all kinds of little

things which these days would be resolved over the telephone. In *loco parentis*, the school needed to check whether this or that was acceptable. My mum would reply with her quiet wisdom and her confidence in both me and the school.

As Albrighton was a very musical school, preparing students to pursue careers as organists, music teachers and piano tuners, there were regular concerts, some by famous professionals, such as Julian Bream and Maria Donska. While I had no desire to follow any of these careers and was no great shakes as a musician, I could get by on a piano, accordion or, my favourite, the melodica, a wind instrument with a keyboard similar to the one on an accordion. My chief musical talent, it has been said, lies in my ability to blow my own trumpet. Be that as it may, classical music has proved a lasting source of pleasure, though, as with poetry, I dislike dissecting it. All too often it seems that poetry and Shakespeare's plays, for instance, are spoilt for children by detailed analysis, when instead they should be experiencing and thereby appreciating the rounded nature of expression and the natural music of the words.

As before, I continued to enjoy the challenge of mental arithmetic. What a pity it is that recent research has shown that children's lack of numeracy can be put down to the fact that calculators have taken over from the use of their brains. Yes, I am a fundamentalist when it comes to education: I believe in discipline, solid mental arithmetic, learning to read and write accurately, plenty of homework, increasing expectations and developing potential – all the things which are anathema to many modern children.

While boarding school tends to make boys tough

and self-reliant, it seldom prepares them for the more sensitive, gentler aspects of life. Practicalities mean that boys have to fend for themselves, often acquiring thick, defensive shells to cope with crowded classrooms and dormitories where, as I have said, there is never any space or privacy. Boys ferret through each other's lockers and know each other's business; in short, everyone interferes. Without the daily love and support of family, pupils can become hardened, fail to mature as rounded individuals and are largely ignorant of how to conduct relationships, particularly with the opposite sex.

While it is true that boys and girls shared classrooms and some activities, such as concerts and play rehearsals, almost every other aspect of life was conducted separately. Naturally, girls' and boys' dormitories were in separate blocks, but so too were our recreation rooms. For a large part of each day we led parallel existences: boys playing cards, listening to records, kicking a football around or chatting in their houses, while, with the exception of football, the girls did much the same in theirs. If boys attempted to enter the girls' recreation room for a chat or to swap records, for instance, they were generally promptly ejected by a member of staff, no matter how innocent the reason for being there. Such strict segregation of the sexes was unwise because, instead of regarding girls merely as objects of sexual interest, we needed to learn how to relax and simply be at ease with girls, how to share with them, even how to express affection in a platonic fashion. Most of us remained clueless about how to handle relationships with the opposite sex and spent far too much time planning how to sneak off into the grounds with a girl for a furtive cuddle.

Of course my early time at Rowton was over-shadowed by my father's death. When my grandfather died three years later, things did not improve and my feelings of frustration that the world was unjust were reinforced by the circumstances of his death. In 1956 Mum was found to be suffering from breast cancer, which was much more life-threatening then than it is today. Indeed it was a tribute to the early National Health Service that she survived not only breast cancer but also other illnesses, including an operation to remove her gall bladder. Finally, after twenty odd years of looking after her father, she could no longer cope physically. Grandad, aged ninety-two, was therefore admitted to the geriatric ward of the Northern General Hospital. In the sixties, residential homes would not take elderly people who were incapable of looking after themselves to some degree. In the nineties this has totally changed and places in homes are only available to those too frail to look after themselves. During the school holidays, I regularly went with Mum to visit Grandad in hospital. No one who has ever visited such a ward can ever forget it. It was a heart-breaking experience. Though clean, the ward was large, gloomy and depressing, dominated at one end by a huge television − another irony, given Grandad's dislike of such appliances. All the old people sat around or were propped up in bed, some trying to converse with each other, some dozing, others going gradually senile. The staffing levels were poor and many had no training. Without wishing to disparage the kindness of those involved, the staff saw their task literally as feeding and putting to bed old people who in a sense had started to become children again. For my mother it was particularly sad because she had given so much of her later life to caring for Grandad, keeping him alert and comfy. In the end he died after falling down some steps in the ward. I swore then that if ever the chance arose to do something to lift people out of such conditions I would seize the opportunity with both hands.

I returned to Rowton Castle with renewed determination to change the world, so that people would not have to end their lives in geriatric wards, not to have to scrimp as Mum was doing, not to have to die needlessly like my father . . . I cannot now pinpoint any single cause for my angry determination, but determined I was, and no less cockily self-confident in other respects.

On a lighter note, I recall protesting vociferously to school staff about the endless Spam and mashed potato we received for our main meal of the day. More decisive was a subsequent campaign: after protracted negotiations, pupils were finally granted permission to wear more than one clean shirt per week. With stuffy classrooms and crowded passageways, the staff cannot have failed to appreciate the benefit of this decision, but I do not suppose they looked upon me as anything but a difficult child, a potential troublemaker.

As a means of distraction I listened for hours to the radio: sports reports, plays, the Paul Temple murder detection serial, *Life with the Lyons*, *The Clitheroe Kid*, and later *Hancock's Half Hour*, *The Navy Lark*, and *Beyond Our Ken* and *Round the Horne* with Kenneth Horne and the outrageous Kenneth Williams. What a pleasurable escape they were. I also already had my season ticket for listening to *The Archers*.

It all started when I was about four. I think it was the music — that is the old music — rather than the country dialogue that caught my fancy. Every night of the week, on what was then the Home Service of the BBC, Mum and I would do a little jig in the confined space of our front room to the signature tune, 'Dum di dum di dum di dum, dum di dum di dum dum . . . ' Mum laughed and I laughed too. I was hooked. Throughout my schooldays I would tune in each evening or catch the Sunday omnibus edition. Old fuddy duddy that I am, it was only when the programme was updated and became a countrified version of north London that I started to lose interest. Gone are the opening remarks of Tom Forrest, former gamekeeper, who used to keep us city folk in touch with the seasons, with what was happening in the countryside, with the changes in the farming calendar and the hibernation of animals and the migration of birds. I still listen, but not as avidly, and not every Sunday addictively as I did in the past.

Gradually, however, I began immersing myself in news and current affairs, reaching out to a world beyond the school confines. Frequently I was to be found with my ear avidly pressed to the transistor radio and from such worthy programmes came most of my knowledge of politics and language; indeed I learned to be reasonably articulate long before I could express myself lucidly on paper.

More importantly, what I heard on the radio and my reading of history encouraged me to become a fully paid-up member of the Labour Party. At sixteen I was not by any means a revolutionary and I was not at that time on the Left of British politics, although all my close family had always been Labour voters. But I wanted to change the world; instinctively I wished to see things improve. All too clearly I recognised what conditions were like where I was brought up, the tragedy of Dad's death, my mother's struggle to survive, how shabbily she had been treated by the Gas Board, and the way my grandfather had ended his days. The lives of our neighbours were not much different. All this combined to make me very angry. Although at that stage I did not have an intellectual focus in terms of values and principles, I had already learned sufficient history to appreciate that through the ages there has been a constant struggle not only between right and wrong but also between those with power and wealth and those who have neither.

Evidently I had no power or wealth, nor had most of the people I had been brought up with, and I wanted to do something to remedy this state of affairs. In 1962–3 Harold Wilson was very persuasive about his vision of the future. There was much talk of the 'white heat of technology', of economic planning, of creating a better world in which to live and a better country in which all could benefit from such developments. It was an exciting decade; people had hope. What makes Britain depressing today is the pervading pessimism about our future and lack of belief that there can be an alternative to deteriorating public services, the dole, violence, shoddy public transport and general indifference to each other's plight. I am still fired deep inside by the same commitment to improve things as when I was a teenager. In my late teens, however, I disliked attending local party meetings because they generally consisted of arguments about the minutes of previous meetings and details which had nothing to do with changing the world. Political structure in terms of local authorities was pretty much a mystery, as it still is for many, but I suspected even then that power lay in Parliament. At the time, I had no thought of making a career in politics other than the vague belief that getting into Parliament must be the way to begin the changes that I wanted to make.

Looking back, 1963 – the year I turned sixteen – seems to have been a pivotal point. It was the year my grandfather died, the year I joined the Labour Party, the year I left Rowton to transfer to the senior, further education branch of the College at Albrighton Hall, and the year I came to the instinctive conclusion that, if I were ever going to rise above low income and under achievement, a sound education with O- and A-level qualifications was crucial.

Dotheboys Hall in *Nicholas Nickleby* springs to mind when I recall my years at Albrighton. Conditions were Spartan and the food so poor that I again led a delegation to protest, this time at being fed sausages four times in one week! Perhaps my attitude might have been tempered had I been able to see the physical charms of the house and its surroundings. Set in the hamlet of Albrighton, which appears in the Domesday Book as belonging to Shrewsbury Abbey, Thomas Ireland, Sheriff of Shropshire, built the Hall of rich red and blue-grey bricks in the Tudor style with large, square rooms and several ornately carved hardwood fireplaces. It must have made a substantial but elegant home when it was completed around 1632. In a field not far away the Battle of Shrewsbury was fought in 1403, and in the seventeenth century more than once Charles I's Royalist forces skirmished with Cromwell's Roundheads in the area. The surroundings added an edge to our scho boy debates on the proposition that 'The Royalists were romantic and wrong, and the Roundheads were repulsive and right'. My heart was with the Royalists, but my head with the Parliamentarians.

Over the following two centuries the Hall changed hands several times and in 1853 it came into the possession of the Sparrow family, who occupied the house until the depredations of thirty Second World War evacuees forced them to sell up. Since then it has been, in turn, a home for nuns, a rehabilitation centre for ex-servicemen, a school for the blind, a training centre for the Trustee Savings Bank, a private home and now it is a smart hotel.

The history of my surroundings was interesting, but no compensation for the fact that, as at Rowton Castle, we were physically cut off from normal social life, being several miles out of town. Buses to Shrewsbury ran infrequently and, again as at Rowton, our days were organised along the lines of the public school system with Wednesday afternoons devoted largely to sports and Saturday mornings to classwork. This system created major constraints in that pupils rarely went home for the weekend and so we had to make our own social life. I liked reading, we played a lot of football, table tennis and cricket, and I did a great deal of walking on my own around the grounds and beyond. Listening to birdsong and the abundant natural life was a joy. It would have been a pleasant environment if we had not been made to feel imprisoned. A regret which rested with me a good many years after leaving school was my failure to enjoy myself, to have fun like everyone else appeared to be doing in the sixties. In an attempt to ginger things up I organised a school sports and social club. Our outings were mostly sporting fixtures against other schools for the blind or against Shrewsbury, the local public school. On visits to the latter we learned about the fagging system and were shown a large open fire, which the boys swore was used only for toasting bread, but we had our doubts. It all seemed too much like *Tom Brown's Schooldays* for comfort.

I enjoyed sharing social activities with close friends,

but we never really let our hair down. At the start of every term, Dr Langdon, the Principal of what was now termed the Royal Normal College and Academy of Music for the Blind, would announce at assembly, 'The local inns are out of bounds,' and smile at his play on words. The nearest pub was about a mile away and not many boys were reckless enough to risk getting caught in such an obvious place. Some did, however, sneak a few drinks at weekends in the taverns of Shrewsbury before leaping on to a bus back to the College. The Principal's prohibition and the school's remoteness from normal family life actually increased the likelihood of boys going for a drink, thinking it a challenge.

Another depressing aspect of moving to Albrighton was that, although Rowton had encouraged us to develop broad general knowledge and a high standard of debate, we had received a poor academic education in terms of English, maths and science, among other subjects. The College aimed to provide further education largely in the form of work-related skills. With such an inadequate formal education thus far, I felt as though I were starting again from scratch and so did a number of classmates. Some of my friends from Rowton days who went with me to evening classes went back into education later on to study computer programming, physiotherapy and such like; but when we were sixteen light engineering was the most common career option for blind youngsters across the country.

At Albrighton I opted to take a commercial course, which consisted of learning braille shorthand and how to use an ordinary typewriter, plus classes in English and some commercial aspects of business studies. The short-hand and typing proved very helpful in terms of study, particularly for essays as well as for communicating. With an ordinary typewriter I could type on regular typing paper or, if multiple copies were required, on waxed stencil sheets. In this way my work became readily accessible to whoever had to scrutinise it. The only drawback was that, if I lost my place or made a mistake, I had to start over again on a fresh line because I would not be able to find my place, as with braille. Nevertheless this new-found skill encouraged a slightly greater sense of freedom of expression. The shorthand typing course was a lengthy one, usually four years, but I completed it in three. The course was structured with the slowest pupil in mind and therefore seemed rather unnecessarily protracted. Our days were filled, but I found it frustrating that the course scarcely stretched us or tapped our full potential. Things are very different nowadays at the equivalent college based at Hereford, where the full range of national exam qualifications are pursued alongside such skills as shorthand and typing.

Inspired at least in part by reading *How Green Was My Valley*, the certainty I felt about the benefits of exams was not shared by Dr Langdon. His view was that exams were unnecessary, that they narrowed academic and intellectual development, and it was therefore a waste of time for pupils to study for them. Such an attitude angers me to this day because he had a PhD. I wonder how he thought he could have become head of a college without qualifications. When I asked why there was no provision for sitting O and A levels, I was informed that he did not 'believe' in them and the curriculum was not geared towards them. Much was to change later when Mr Lidster took over as Principal, but at that time Dr Langdon's answer was tantamount to a challenge, not only to me but also to five of my classmates. We decided to enrol for evening classes at the local Technical College in Shrewsbury, three miles away, and after much pressure Dr Langdon granted permission for us to attend. For over a year or more no transport was provided and we had to catch infrequent local buses to and fro. On cold, wet evenings, making our way there and back again late at night was hard. Only the conviction that exams were the sole means of making something of ourselves drove us on.

We were a motley crew. Tony Randall, argumentative and strong-willed, was in many respects similar in character to myself, if not even slightly more abrasive. (I hope Tony will not take offence at this. If he does, we can have a good argument about it!) He is now a senior computer analyst for Marks & Spencer in London. Graeme McCreath, strong and wiry, spent a large amount of time weight-lifting, an activity he still pursues over twenty-five years on. He now lives in Victoria on Vancouver Island, Canada, where he works as a physiotherapist. Geoff Bashton, also small and wiry, went on from Albrighton to a Jewish sixth-form college in London and rose to become a senior adviser in the Department of Health. David Boyce, an immense charmer with girls, became a close friend, although he had no interest in politics. After leaving Albrighton, he did an Open University course and a spell as a piano tuner before moving with his family to Sheffield, where he attended the Polytechnic. He went on to take an MA in social work at Nottingham University before moving to Ontario, Canada, where he now lives with his Canadian wife. The fifth member of our group was Roger Williams, a big, strong lad from Bristol, who was very bumptious and far preferred having a bit of fun to studying. He went on to become a telephonist and typist for a bank, and was last heard of doing computer studies.

The six of us, comrades in arms, struggled to keep each other up to the mark, not only attending classes but doing homework too. We saw it as a collective challenge – to study while other boarders were larking about, playing cards or football, listening to the radio or their records. It was so tempting merely to put our feet up in the lounge, listen to a favourite programme and have a smoke. There was no academic ethos, and it was difficult to find a quiet place to study. We had to make space physically, as well as in terms of time, since the dormitories housed eight boys and there were no study rooms. Sometimes a music practice room might be empty or a secluded corner of the school grounds in summer. Had I not successfully passed the two o levels I sat during that first year, I might not have carried on. As it was, having achieved success, the realisation that I might make it became a strong incentive. I suppose the drive to prove something to myself as well as to others has kept me going all my life. Each step encourages me to go further, as does the knowledge that I have the capacity and intellect to achieve a given task. I still strive, sometimes too hard, to demonstrate that I can match anything anyone else can do. There are those even today who are reluctant to admit to themselves that a blind person is quite capable of working with them on equal terms, or might possibly do the job better.

After the first difficult year, Wilf King from Rowton Castle volunteered to meet us at the tech'. He went to a great deal of trouble – sometimes falling asleep after a hard day's work while we were at the classes – and he gave us much moral support. It would be unfair, however, to give the impression that Wilf was the sole person to encourage us. There was one other, rather special person: Margaret Waddington. An elderly, retired schoolmistress, she came to the College part-time to teach English for the Commerce course. She was a lovely lady and at first despaired of our class because we were such a rowdy bunch. Nevertheless, when she discovered that I loved poetry, she warmed to me. Then, one day, I struck lucky. After reading a poem to us, she asked, 'Does anybody know who wrote that?' I have no idea why, but I took a calculated guess. 'Keats,' I piped up. Mrs Waddington was immensely surprised to receive the correct answer. Encouraged to believe there might after all be something between our ears, she generously agreed to give me and my five buddies extra tuition in grammar and comprehension for the 0-level English Language paper.

Thus it came about that over the following three years at evening classes I took two 0 levels per year – History and English Language, Geography and Commerce, Religious Knowledge and, almost suicidally, Physics plus A-level Economics. To this day I am not certain how I passed Physics. Gradually, from classes and various written sources, I learned enough technical language to get through the exam paper. Fortunately, instead of having to draw experiments, I was permitted to describe them, which was a great boon. If I did not know the precise answer, I was able to phrase a response in an ambiguous way, in the hope that the examiner might give me the benefit of the doubt. In retrospect this, too, seems to have been a useful preparation for life in politics.

Religious Knowledge was a less taxing exam subject since, whenever I was home in Sheffield, Mum and

I regularly attended weekly services at the local Methodist church. Psalms, hymns and other poetic passages in the Bible had particular appeal, and I was for many years sincerely interested in religion.

Learning foreign languages was not a high priority on our curriculum, presumably because College staff felt, with some justification, that pupils had enough trouble mastering English, let alone French or German. This omission became particularly evident when one of our women teachers and a local youth club leader, who were going out together, jointly organised a week-long trip to Paris for a group of sighted and blind young people. Immediately I heard of this, I was keen to go – my first holiday abroad. I began to dream about this romantic city, full of the history and culture that we had only just begun to learn about. Remarkably my mother agreed to use some of the compensation awarded for Dad's death to fund me.

As it transpired, our week in Paris was anything but romantic. Our accommodation in a school cum orphanage on the periphery of the city was Spartan. The food, although our first introduction to French cooking, was hardly *haute cuisine*. On several days, the whole group travelled into the centre of Paris by Métro to explore, and I remember David Boyce and I took a rowing boat out on a lake, which was presumably the equivalent of London's Serpentine. I enjoyed strolling along the cobbled streets, taking in the foreign sounds and smells, good and bad. We ordered *citron pressés*, fresh lemon juice with sugar and ice, from the small street bars, and I felt quite grown-up. I have a rather less pleasant memory of a visit to a public swimming pool and bathhouse, where the man in front of me in the queue had all too evidently come for a bath rather than to swim. I remember wondering at the time how Frenchmen came to have such a romantic image. This was also my first encounter with the appalling state of French public lavatories, which I have to say I found decidedly less funny than I did years later, when I thoroughly enjoyed the BBC television series *Clochemerle* screened in the early seventies. Another incident which struck me was when the members of our group who could see were taken off to visit the Louvre, while we College boys were not. I suppose the organisers believed touring an art gallery would be wasted on us, whereas in fact, with helpful description, it is possible for paintings to be brought alive and made meaningful. In those days visitors with impaired sight were not allowed to touch the sculptures in the way they are encouraged to do today. All in all, however, I revelled in the novel experiences, tastes and smells of that trip to Paris and later spent hours reminiscing with David Boyce and the others.

One of the problems with being away from home, as well as being at a school where Saturday mornings were timetabled as part of the working week, was the inability to join in normal social activities. One such event was the FA Cup Final of 1966. Even if I had been at home, I know it would have been enormously difficult to obtain a ticket and even more difficult for me to get to Wembley – presumably on my own – but in 1966 I was stuck listening to Sheffield Wednesday v Everton on the radio. Raymond Glendenning was one of those commentators who could make a match come alive, without being over the top. These days, commentators often exaggerate any move to goal, leading to disappointment when the final touch goes astray. On this wonderful sunny afternoon in May I sat overlooking the lake at Albrighton Hall, listening as Sheffield Wednesday went 2–0 up. I could not believe it. I was on my feet pacing up and down in front of the seat where I had deposited myself and my portable radio. The sun continued to shine, but clouds began to gather as Everton first scored one, then two and at last, to my great disappointment, went into the lead about fifteen minutes from the end.

In 1991 and again in 1993 I would visit Wembley with Sheffield Wednesday, but I shall never forget the disappointment of that sunny afternoon as Sheffield Wednesday in the year of England's World Cup victory lost the game they should have won against all the odds.

When we started attending evening classes, I guess at the back of our minds was the idea that afterwards there might be time to linger in Shrewsbury for a drink; we might even meet some girls. Unfortunately, because the tech' was on the opposite side of town to Albrighton, there was no opportunity for such social experiences. Classes finished at 9PM and it took the best part of an hour to get to the spot where we caught the last bus back to school at 10PM. Week after week we wended our way back and forth to the tech' with never the chance to down a half pint, let alone chat up a girl.

Trips to town, whether in daylight or at night, sometimes resulted in embarrassing moments, especially if I went alone. Quite frequently, when I paused at a kerb, someone would grab my arm and steer me across the street, lifting me bodily up the kerb the other side, without so much as a by your leave. They did so with the best intentions, naturally, but it was irritating to find myself suddenly sailing across the road, particularly if I was actually intending to head off in another direction.

On occasion I was not even certain where I had landed! All blind people have to learn how to deal with such situations and with regret I have to admit that I sometimes overreacted and became quite sharp. The problem is that such overreaction can cause a negative response and the next time that person spots a blind man or woman trying to cross the road, they may not offer to help for fear of being rebuked. I had to learn that sighted people do not always know how best to offer assistance or how to deal with blind people generally.

As a child, people often asked my parents a question which should have been addressed to me, such as 'Does he want a sweet?' or 'Would he like to go and play in the garden?' On these occasions, I felt like declaring 'I am not deaf as well as blind'. The choice of title for the Radio 4 programme for disabled people *Does He Take Sugar?* picks up on this admirably. Sometimes when people first realised I was blind, they would murmur, 'Oh, isn't it a shame', or to me, 'Don't you wish you could see?' Few realise how hurtful such remarks can be. Within the school we were protected from such experiences, but in fact it would have been helpful if there had been some guidance or discussion about how to deal with such situations and how to conduct relationships.

I was, therefore, totally unprepared for a particularly unpleasant experience which occurred one day in Shrewsbury. Walking along the pavement, I could hear two people approaching – an adult and a small child. As their footsteps drew nearer, I heard the woman say to her child, 'Come away, let's cross the road – that boy's blind.' My interpretation at the time was that she evidently believed that blindness was some form of contagious disease, and for a while afterwards I brooded about the incident. Gradually, however, like most blind people, I learned to cope with a wide variety of behaviour and attitudes directed towards me: how to accept unwanted help politely or how to put sighted people at ease in their dealings with me. But it takes time and understanding – on both sides. It is a two-way process, but as a matter of survival, a blind person has to be the first to learn, or risk missing out on making friends or receiving much-valued practical, everyday help.

Following such a rare unpleasant encounter in town, I would return to College angry and depressed. I was pig-headed enough not to let such incidents bother me for long and I would soon bounce back. However, it would be easy for other young people, at such a sensitive age, to retreat into their shells and not venture out as often or as confidently as they would otherwise have done.

It must also have been around this time that a new physical education teacher joined the staff of the College after leaving the Army. One Sunday evening a group of us seventeen- and eighteen-year-olds were relaxing in the lounge. In walked the PE teacher and ordered us off to bed forthwith, accusing us of being too rowdy. As it was only 9PM, we were naturally affronted at being treated like children so, when he left, we decided to get out some hymn books and render a few old favourites at the top of our voices. What could be more saintly on a Sunday evening? Of course, the PE teacher returned and ordered us to stop. When we refused, he stormed off to find the Principal and returned with him a few minutes later, demanding that strong action be taken. As a result, three students were actually suspended from the College and several of us were severely punished by being gated for an entire term, with the threat of suspension or expulsion if we misbehaved in the interim. All this because of what we considered to be a minor incident. Resentment simmered for months.

Given that boarders at Albrighton were between the ages of sixteen and twenty, the fact that this part of the College was single sex was a potential problem. Even though Albrighton was nearer Shrewsbury than Rowton Castle was, it was not easy for us to mix, and the lack of organised events and activities, even with the local youth club, meant that our socialising was very limited. I experienced no overt homosexuality at Albrighton Hall, although it undoubtedly existed in such an exclusively male environment with so many young men cooped up together month after month. Many of my classmates longed, as I did, to interact with a broader spectrum of people who, so the radio and television informed us, were out there enjoying the Swinging Sixties. Much of our knowledge about relationships between men and women was garnered from radio plays, but obviously these were often over-stated and did not always reflect real life. Our source of information was therefore most unreliable as a form of guidance.

To overcome feelings of isolation, several of us joined a Sunday afternoon youth club run by Shrewsbury Methodist Church. To break the ice, I took with me a pack of playing cards. Casually holding them fanned out in one hand, I challenged one of the lads to whom I was introduced to choose one, look at its face value and return it to the pack behind my back; I would then tell the assembled group what card it was. The trick proved highly effective and it was several weeks before anyone guessed that the cards were marked in braille. In the meantime I was the focus of much undeserved praise and attention, which I enjoyed immensely!

The chief attraction of the Methodist youth club meetings and of the church service in the morning was, of course, the large number of girls who attended. From time to time, other youth organisations in the district would also invite a bunch of college students for tea or to a meeting. It was in response to one such invitation that I found myself spending a Sunday afternoon with the members of the Congregational Church in Pontesbury, near Shrewsbury. There I fell into conversation with a girl named Pamela Edwards. As we both stood up to leave at the end of the session, I realised that unless I said something swiftly, there would be no chance of seeing her again.

My intention was to ask her if she would like to go to the cinema with me, but so nervous was I that instead I heard myself blurting out, 'Would you like to come and look round the College at Albrighton?' It was a strange way of asking for a date but to my immense relief she accepted. Several days later, as we walked round the school grounds, at last I plucked up the courage to suggest a visit to the cinema. She said yes.

Pamela was a lively girl with a quick mind. She had left school at sixteen and worked at the local Silhouette factory, making women's underwear. She lived with her parents in a small village to the south of Shrewsbury. Her father suffered from chronic bronchitis and was unable to work, so she and her brother, Alan, supported the family, which included her small brother, David. There was obviously little money to spare, but they were kind enough to offer me hospitality at the weekends, for which I will always be grateful. I know that the extra mouth to feed sometimes caused a problem because the money had to be found from somewhere to cover the cost of my meal.

Pam and I spent many happy times together, going for walks by the river where the boys from the public school practised their rowing, and visiting the cinema which also doubled as the local theatre. I remember Frankie Howerd appearing along with other stars of the time. Pamela made me feel special, that I deserved to respect myself and that I could lead a normal life. Looking back, I realise that my Methodist upbringing, lack of experience with girls and a serious commitment to passing my exams at evening classes meant that I was not the most worldly boyfriend she might have had, but suffice it to say that with Pamela I learned how to kiss and cuddle.

We had been together for about a year when Pamela broke off our relationship in order to go out with an older man who had a car and was able to take her to the pop concerts and shows in Birmingham which appealed to her. I used to wonder what had happened to her and whether she ever saw me on the television, but I recently discovered that she has been living in France for the past ten years, so it is unlikely. However, I hope she remembers our time together with affection.

I do not know if I was in love with Pamela, but I remember being extremely upset when we parted. For a time the experience made me feel that it was virtually impossible, without sight, to compete on the same footing as other young men. I felt a deep sense of rejection. In an effort to raise my spirits, a well-meaning woman at the youth club said there was a girl in a wheelchair whom I ought to meet – she could act as my eyes and I could act as her legs, she said. How insensitive people can be!

For some time afterwards I felt very downhearted and had to make a real effort to lift myself. I had been through a similar period in my early days at Albrighton, before I began attending evening classes and working towards my examinations, when life seemed to be passing me by. I would get up in the morning and ask myself 'What the hell is it all for?' I found living in a boarding-school environment at that age very stultifying. There seemed to be no one in whom I could confide or who could give me reliable advice. Sharing a dormitory with seven others did not give us the privacy we all needed to think things through and grow up. Every now and then one of the boys from the dorm would get drunk and we would look after him. We helped and protected each other in that sort of way, but intimate discussion about emotions was unthinkable. In order to escape I would row a leaky old boat all of fifty feet or so across the ornamental lake in the grounds and take refuge on the tiny island at its centre. Having tied up the boat, I would settle down out of sight behind a bit of shrubbery, with my radio beside me, and stay there for hours, keeping myself to myself. Occasionally I pondered what career I might pursue.

My interest in politics and current affairs led me to believe that one possible career might be in journalism, although I had no idea exactly what this involved. The difference between the reporter going down to the local court room or town or county hall and the leader writer sitting back and reflecting on the week's political events had not yet registered.

So it was, with hope in my heart, I wrote off to the editor of the *Sheffield Morning Telegraph*, then a thriving regional daily newspaper, now reborn as a weekly. I explained that I wished to become a journalist and write leaders or feature articles. The editor responded with a kindly letter, but its content came as a rude awakening. Apparently I could not join his or any other paper at such a senior level; everyone has to start as a junior reporter doing the rounds of weddings, funerals and fêtes. In addition he said he preferred applicants who had completed a journalism course. This was very disappointing.

What was interesting about the reply, and the College raised the issue separately on my behalf, was the way in which he assumed that a blind person could not be a journalist. In fact things were easier then than they are now. While there is no problem using braille short-hand or a typewriter or word processor, there are considerable difficulties for blind people using screens, now commonplace on national newspapers. It can be done, but it is slower and undoubtedly more stressful because nowadays journalists have to write their articles to fit the space on the screen in front of the them, rather than leaving the final extent to a sub-editor. Life is, of course, a lot easier the further up the ladder you go; those who write editorials are in an altogether different ball game.

All too frequently other people make a judgement about what is possible rather than looking for ways round a difficulty and helping overcome the obstacles. In fact, journalism and politics have a good deal in common and both can suffer the same fate in public esteem.

I learned two important things from this episode: firstly, that I must learn to express myself through the written word as well as verbally, and secondly, that I did not want to write about other people's activities anyway – I wanted to be active myself.

With this in mind and to celebrate our graduation from Albrighton in August 1967, David Boyce and I scraped enough money together to pay for a pony-trekking holiday on the Isle of Skye. This is not perhaps the most likely destination for two young men of twenty, but for us Skye had an irresistibly romantic aura . . . 'over the sea to Skye', the far north-west, the isolation, the history, the warmth of the Gulf Stream, the atmosphere of epic adventure . . . No one had warned us that August is a dreadful month for midges, that it is more likely to pour with rain than bake in sunshine or that the journey would be complex, long and exhausting. In the event it took the best part of twenty-four hours: on the train from Sheffield to Glasgow, where we changed to a local train for Mallaig, from there by ferry to Armadale and then right up the island by bus to Dunvegan. As so often happens, getting there turned out to be quite an adventure in itself.

David was a great one for chatting up girls, so when two came to share our compartment on the train to Mallaig, I expected him to make a killing, but it transpired they were heading for the Isle of Lewis. In the course of conversation, however, I can distinctly recall one of the girls confiding, 'My name is Denise – it's French, you know,' and David responding quick as a flash, 'My name's David – it's Jewish.' His rejoinder impressed me since he had no Jewish connections.

Alighting at the station in Mallaig, we strode confidently across the quayside to find the ferry. As both my hands were full of luggage, I was unable to use a white cane, and suddenly David, who could see a little, yelled, 'Stop!' I stopped dead. Apparently my feet were only a few inches from the edge of the quay. Had I toppled over, twenty feet down into the harbour and lost our baggage, the holiday would have been over before it had scarcely begun.

When at last we arrived at Dunvegan, we were disconcerted to find ourselves in a hotel the like of which we had never experienced before. We suspected our clothes were not smart enough for the rather formal atmosphere, and that evening in the dining room we were presented with a four-course meal plus coffee, which seemed very grand. Seeing we were totally non-plussed over which knife and fork to use, the friendly hotel staff inveigled the head of the pony-trekking firm to join us at our table and provide some tactful guidance on etiquette. Looking back, I wonder what other *faux pas* we committed. We were both rather brash and noisy, and perhaps because of this David and I were allocated a room in the annexe. Typically, I wanted a room in the hotel proper and I pestered the staff until, at the end of the first week, our rooms were changed for nicer ones in the main building. David was slightly disappointed at this turn of events, since it removed him from the close proximity of a girl he was hotly pursuing.

If the hotel surprised us, so too did the sea, which, despite the Gulf Stream, turned out to be extremely cold. This did not deter us, though, from taking a rowing boat out on the loch by ourselves, a rash move given David's limited eyesight and the fact that the loch was, of course, tidal. We might so easily never have set foot on dry land again. That we should have taken such a risk says much about our characters.

Pony-trekking, too, provided its share of thrills. David's mount seemed bent on trotting beneath the lowest tree branches it could find in order to sweep him from the saddle. Fortunately he had learned how to fall without injuring himself in judo classes at College. My pony, I was relieved to discover, was far more amenable and I had a wonderful time trotting over bogs and beaches of fine sand. No pollution, no noise, no crowds – what heaven! When not riding, we tramped for miles on roads which bounced as we walked because of the peat beneath them. We gave a friendly shout to anyone who passed us in a car, urging them to join us in the glorious fresh air.

Our fortnight on Skye was very different from what we had expected, but we loved it just the same and were sorry to leave. Shortly before our departure, I was given a six-pound salmon, which I was determined to take home to my mother, despite advice to the contrary. On the trains home the fish proved a positive boon, for as soon as anyone opened the door of our small compartment, the smell, which was as pungent as ripe Gorgonzola, drove them away instantly, leaving space to ourselves. Mum, too, had reservations about the salmon when I presented it to her with the request that she cook it for us to eat that evening.

4

TEA CEREMONIES

'SIT DOWN AND have a cup of tea,' said my mother in her most down-to-earth manner. It was a moment of high tension. The postman had just delivered an envelope containing my examination results. I had passed not only the tests for shorthand at 110 words per minute and Stage Three typewriting but also my final two GCE O-levels and – against all expectations – A-level Economics. The excitement of being presented with the Guy Campbell Prize for Physical Education on my final Sports Day at Albrighton a few weeks earlier paled into insignificance. These results were to be my springboard for the future.

The most important thing my mother ever taught me was to love and care for others; the second was 'You are as good as anyone else'. So effectively had she boosted my morale over the years, however, that periodically she felt the need to take me down a peg or two. This was just such an occasion. 'I've passed them all,' I gasped, as I grabbed her hands. 'Sit down and have a cup of tea' was her way of saying, 'Take it in your stride, son, don't get too big for your boots'. But the pride and relief I felt at that moment made my spirits soar.

I had just turned nineteen, and boarding school with its mixed memories was at last behind me. It was the summer of 1967 and I felt the world was my oyster. Gradually, though, I began to calm down and become more thoughtful. The College had, after all, provided a protected environment; while I was not sorry to leave, the future was rather daunting. I was about to take a leap into the unknown. Having been away at school, I had no friends of my own age in Sheffield and no longer felt part of the local community. But I had had enough of boarding school, I was a grown man, and now was the moment to take up the challenge of trying to earn a living. However, I did miss my friends at school and certainly remember worrying that I might be left on the shelf. Such anxieties may seem typical of most teenagers but I was no longer sixteen. I was almost twenty, although intellectually and emotionally much younger. In terms of social experience I felt years behind the times and my career prospects were distinctly uncertain.

Journalism had been ruled out, but teaching appealed. I was unsure about how to proceed. Shortly before leaving the Royal Normal College, the Careers Officer of the Royal National Institute for the Blind, whose responsibility it was to help place youngsters, virtually made the decision for me. I would have preferred the help of normal employment services because there was a tendency by the RNIB to appeal to sentiment. In the event, the Careers Officer approached the East Midlands Gas Board, both on this basis and on the grounds that my father had been killed while in their employ. They had little option but to take me on. Of course I was glad of the job as a clerk typist on a wage of £12 per week, but I found the situation embarrassing and it was a less than ideal start to my working life. What the RNIB officer apparently failed to understand was that self-esteem and confidence are built through genuine achievement and merit rather than patronage. Nevertheless I knew I was fortunate to be able to earn a wage, so I swallowed my pride and went to work in the Gas Board's administration offices. Once safely installed, I not only became a shop steward but I also persuaded the powers that be to let me have day-release to attend the local college of further education. Each week a full day and one evening were spent studying for the National Certificate in Business Studies, while a second evening was devoted to A-level Economic History, which I really enjoyed. Having passed A-level Economic History with grade B and resat A-level Economics to gain a higher grade, I then took A-level Law.

It was not long after I had started work at the East Midlands Gas Board that I took part in what must be my strangest ever television appearance. I have to say at this point that those producing the programme showed exemplary behaviour under what must have seemed at the time considerable provocation. Events unfolded in a way which today seem quite bizarre, but at the time a combination of strong opinions and prudishness drove me into action.

The BBC had run a programme the exact details of which now escape me, but the producer was a then very young David Dimbleby and I had been watching the programme with my Mum. What had caused offence and was commented on in the media was the portrayal of naked bodies lying in a morgue. It was, in fact, a current affairs programme and today no one would bat an eyelid at such scenes, but, despite the fact that we were in the Swinging Sixties, sensitivities were greater than they are today.

Two things struck me. Firstly the fact that nakedness was being shown on prime-time television. Secondly that the dignity of the deceased and their families was being infringed. I put typeface to paper and off went my letter of protest to a viewers' concerns programme chaired by David Coleman, later of *Sportsnight*.

A telephone call came from the BBC. Would it be possible for me to come to London to appear live on the programme? Never one to duck a challenge, I agreed, and, having chatted over the telephone, they were obviously convinced that I would be able to hold my own on the programme. Incidentally, I had never mentioned to them that I was blind.

So it was that I arrived, white stick in hand, at BBC Television Centre. I did not need to see their faces; I could actually feel the sheer bewilderment, nay horror, as they greeted me. Here was a young blind man about to appear on their programme to comment on the filming of naked bodies in a morgue, which he could not possibly have seen, but which somehow had given him great offence. At this point I think it important to indicate that, if actually seeing something were the crucial factor in my making a judgement about whether or not it is appropriate, there is little in life I would actually comment on, but for some people it remains a mystery that I am able to make appropriate and balanced judgements about such matters.

In any event I persuaded them that I wanted to appear on the programme and, seated next to a repre-sentative of Mary Whitehouse's Listeners' and Viewers' Association, I gave as good as I got. David Dimbleby, defending his programme, did not pull any punches and neither did I. I think I lost on points, but I made my stand and argued, as I have over so many years, against the philosophy that 'anything goes'. While I declined Mrs Whitehouse's invitation to join the Listeners' and Viewers' Association and become involved with their campaigns, I learned one or two useful lessons.

I was to learn another before the night was out. I had been put up by the BBC in what was, in retrospect, a pretty seedy hotel for my overnight stay. At about two o'clock in the morning, I called the reception desk to ask if anything could be done about the two men obviously having a petulant lovers' quarrel beneath my window; they were throwing bottles and cans, and one of them even burst into tears. 'I am afraid we do have some problems with drug-takers,' came the terse reply from the desk. This was, after all, London in the Swinging Sixties.

All work and no play makes Jack, let alone David, a dull boy, I thought, as I pursued what swiftly became a daily round of home, routine office chores and intensive course studies. No doubt it was boredom and frustration which drove me, in the spring of 1968, to embark on one of my more foolhardy ventures. It may not now seem particularly challenging when viewed thirty years on but it certainly seemed so at the time. Much against my mother's will, I determined to go on my own to London to the FA Cup quarter final between Chelsea and Sheffield Wednesday at Stamford Bridge. The idea, daft as it may seem on reflection, was that I would meet my old schoolfriend Tony Randall, who could see a little, outside the ground, before going in together.

The challenge was to catch the coach from the bus station in Sheffield, make my way from the drop-off point in London and then find Tony outside the main gate. Looking back, I like to think it was our naivety, rather than stupidity, which carried us through. Having successfully found the right coach, I settled myself with a friendly crowd of Sheffield Wednesday supporters, who gave me a hand at the motorway service station and also accompanied me as we walked to the stadium. It was not until I reached the ground that the thought occurred that finding Tony might be a problem. Then the enormity of the task I had set myself hit me. Here I was in a crowd of thousands of people, all milling around, without a clue what Tony looked like. How could I describe him to anyone so that they might help me locate him? Equally, how was Tony going to decide where to stand outside the gates and how did he think he was going to manage to pick me out when he could see only a yard or two in front of him?

This is where the gods intervened. The Sheffield Wednesday symbol is an owl; somehow its wisdom and ability to see in the dark ruled supreme. From somewhere above the din of thousands of fans a voice rang out – and there he was, my old friend Tony.

As for the match itself, we commandeered someone behind us to give us a running commentary, which I now realise was a bit of a cheek. Honours were even at 1–1. Only then did I come face to face with the prospect of having to find the coach to get home again. On this occasion, the experience of asking people for help and finding that they appeared to make a considerable detour, sometimes to the edge of the pavement, in order to avoid me, gave me my first real taste of what life would be like later on in London. I eventually met up again with a crowd of Sheffield Wednesday supporters and found the coach just in time to avoid being stranded. On the way home I reflected that perhaps in future I might err on the side of caution in finding a balance between independence and foolishness.

Despite such adventures, I still felt my life was falling into a rut as I never seemed to have the opportunity to meet new people. Strange as it may seem, in addition to being socially awkward, I suffered at that time from a minor touch of agoraphobia. This meant I had to pluck up courage and literally grit my teeth in order to climb on a bus and find a seat, so sure was I that everyone must be looking at me. But, despite all this and the fear of making a fool of myself, I determined to try to make some friends by joining the local Methodist youth club. I consoled myself with the thought that at least I would probably know some of the adults supervising the club since it was attached to the church which Mum and I attended.

Not surprisingly, perhaps, the supervisor was rather more welcoming than the members who stood around in close-knit groups. As a newcomer, I felt left out. At most sessions, however, once the music started and people began dancing, the atmosphere improved, but unfortunately dancing is not my forte. Sight plays a vital part in learning how to dance because it is essential to be able to see what people are doing in order to copy the steps and join in, otherwise it is left to the imagination. I did make valiant efforts in this direction but never quite managed to learn to jive confidently.

While the others leapt about to records by the Rolling Stones or numbers from the Beatles' aptly titled album, *Sergeant Pepper's Lonely Hearts Club Band*, for the most part I stood on the sidelines, tapping a foot to the beat. The thought of asking a girl to dance was nerve-wracking, but nevertheless one evening I plucked up courage and walked over to ask someone. 'No, thank you very much,' came the gruff voice of a male. I could feel the heat rising from my shirt collar to my cheeks and up my forehead as I made a desperate effort to turn away with my dignity intact. I retreated to gather my shattered pride and what was left of my self-confidence. Trudging home that evening with my heart in my boots, I wondered how I could ever set foot in the youth club again.

Life seemed to comprise one long series of pitfalls from which I always emerged with egg on my face. No one likes to make a fool of himself in public, but blind people feel particularly vulnerable and concerned to preserve their dignity. It must have been around this same time that, in the course of an office meeting with colleagues, I needed to leave an unfamiliar room to fetch some papers in a hurry. If I had had a guide dog, I would simply have told it to find the door. Instead, I followed standard practice and walked briskly along the wall with hand outstretched until I felt the door. Saying 'I won't be long', I turned the doorknob and stepped straight in to a broom cupboard. The stuff of Whitehall farce, I can laugh about it now and might even consider pretending to do such a thing in jest, but at the time I found it deeply embarrassing. The indignity made me want to retreat into myself and stay at home.

Only sheer bloody-minded stubbornness made me turn up for the next session at the youth club. I refused to be defeated. The others at the club could have had no inkling of how hard it was to force myself to walk in through the door and join them in the hall.

It was not at the youth club, though, that I first met Ruth Mitchell, but at one of the sessions held after Sunday evening chapel. These were discussion groups, where I did not feel an outsider but joined in enthusiastically and held my own, speaking, thinking and contributing on equal terms, just like everyone else. In 1968, Ruth was seventeen, in the sixth form of a girls' grammar school on the south-west side of Sheffield and lived with her parents on Longley Lane, about a mile and a half from Parson Cross.

Ruth's mother, a keen churchgoer who had transferred from the Baptist to the Methodist Church, was a full-time housewife, while her father, an engineer by profession, was Deputy Head of Rotherham College of Technology. She had a younger sister, Anne, who later went on to study Physics and became a teacher.

At the discussion groups Ruth and I would say hello and sometimes pass the time of day. Then, one evening as I left the office, I found her waiting for me outside. Most days thereafter, when she came out of school, she would come to meet me after work. On the bus home we talked, or rather Ruth would talk – without stopping to draw breath. Given my own propensity for talking a lot, this did not seem unduly strange, although it did lead me to experience uncharacteristic bouts of silence.

Ruth was short and stocky with long hair, which I found attractive. I liked her because she seemed prepared to help and keep me company, and because she was undeterred by my blindness. Rather the reverse in fact: I think she thought I was manageable. Eventually I asked her out to the cinema and was surprised to discover she had only been once in her life. In terms of going out with friends of her own age to enjoy herself, Ruth's experience was even more limited than mine. In her company I felt more worldly wise than I truly was. Her puzzling lack of social experience appealed to me and presented a challenge. I would have liked to have taken her to some of Sheffield's emerging variety clubs to enjoy dinner and a show, but she was not interested in that sort of thing. Instead we went for walks, to the cinema or church youth sessions and generally spent quiet evenings together.

I was working very hard and was by nature serious, certainly no bundle of fun, a characteristic which I know had put off Pamela. Ruth's parents were ambivalent about her going out with me, mainly because of my politics and apparent lack of career prospects at the time. On the face of it, my future did not seem promising – a blind man with a few qualifications, attending day-release classes while working as a Gas Board clerk typist. At that stage there did not seem much hope, except in my heart. We never discussed my blindness, but, like any parents, they must have been concerned. Ignoring our parents' reservations, Ruth and I continued to meet.

Ruth was studying for A-levels and was unhappy with one of her subjects, English Literature, so I suggested she switch to Modern Economic History, covering the same syllabus I had just completed, and I offered to help her with it. Thus it came about that our main shared activity was working: she would read me material I was studying on the National Certificate course, while I would offer advice on her course work. In the event, Ruth gained a grade A in the exam, so I felt I had done a good job and was pleased for her. These shared interests drew us together and over a period of time made us increasingly dependent on each other for support and companionship.

There was, however, another potential relationship on my mind at this period. Following the break-up with Pamela, I had decided to acquire a penfriend, preferably one who lived somewhere exotic. I had been writing to Maria Salerno, who lived in Malta, which, though not wildly exotic, had the advantage that I could write in English rather than in the small amount of Esperanto I had learned at College. Letters flowed regularly to and fro until at last I was invited by Maria's parents to visit Malta in the summer of 1968. I suspect Maria and her family, influenced by the fact that I had written to her from College, had originally wondered whether I might make a suitable spouse. The problem is, of course, that correspondents can easily develop a picture of each other which bears little resemblance to reality. Although I had alerted them to the fact, until I arrived in Malta I do not think that the Salernos fully understood that I could not see. Only then did the enormity hit them. Here was a struggling office clerk with few prospects to offer their cherished daughter.

Instead of staying in the family home, as I had expected, I found myself boarding with a nice couple originally from Lincolnshire, Eileen and Neil Doggett. Neil was a driver with the RAF. Although Maria and I were chaperoned everywhere we went, the Salernos became increasingly concerned about a relationship developing between us. As a consequence, I was forced to spend more and more time with the Doggetts. It was an awkward situation, since they must have felt that I had been thrust upon them. Nevertheless they were very welcoming and showed me the island. In any case, there was the hot sunshine, warm sea and sandy beaches to enjoy and by the end of the fortnight I had come to like Malta and the Doggetts so much that, in spite of the embarrassing situation regarding the Salernos, I vowed to return the following year.

Throughout the cold and gloom of a Sheffield winter the golden climate of Malta beckoned. So keen was I to return that my enthusiasm infected Ruth, who reluctantly agreed to accompany me. Unfortunately this turned out to be a serious mistake. The hot weather was a misery to her. I found I did not want to do the things she wanted to do and she did not like what I liked. We fell out repeatedly; the only thing we agreed on was the fact that the trip had turned out to be a disaster. This should have been a warning to us both in terms of our future prospects together.

Back in Sheffield once more my job at the Gas Board grew less stimulating as the months passed, despite my union work. At home, Mum and I would sit by the fire sometimes, discussing what I might do once all the exams were over. My mother believed that controversy and conflict over politics and religion were very dangerous, and that careers in these fields should be avoided at all costs. I suspected she was right, but I was keenly interested in both.

During the final year at Albrighton, a careers and recruitment man suggested I might train as a Methodist minister. In my early twenties it was still an option and I became a local preacher (equivalent to a lay preacher in the Church of England). As such I learned to conduct church services in lieu of absent ministers on the local Methodist circuit. Congregations must have regarded me as a bit of a radical, talking politics in the pulpit, much as the Nonconformists had in the late-nineteenth century. I did not preach Party politics, but in a world where controversy is politics and the establishment is the norm, it was politics nonetheless. Working as a local preacher was no mere cynical exercise in public speaking, although admittedly it was splendid practice. While my shyness was debilitating in most social situations, it seemed to evaporate in a pulpit or on a speaker's podium, partly because I felt in control of the situation and partly because I was incredibly opinionated and truly believed I had something important to impart.

After a while, however, it became apparent that my temperament did not suit the ministry, and in later years formal religion ceased to seem relevant to me. While I have never rejected faith, I believe in a Life Force, a force for good and evil, not a tangible being. The only way I can describe it is that, rather like electricity, we need to discover how to draw on and utilise that power. While some people can draw on the power of good, there are obviously those who are able to draw on the power of evil. There are forces at work few fully comprehend. If I had the time to do so, this is an area I would like to examine much more closely.

As for my mother's other *bête noire*, politics, my joining the Labour Party in Shrewsbury at sixteen had not met with her wholehearted approval. Nor was she best pleased when, shortly after returning to Sheffield, I decided to become active in the local party. I distinctly remember setting off on my own across the large council estate of Parson Cross to seek out the wooden community hut in which the Southey Green Ward branch of the Labour Party held its meetings.

When I arrived, I found a couple of people standing outside the door. 'Can't we go in?' I asked.

'No,' someone replied, 'the secretary's forgotten the key. He's gone back home to get it.'

A few more people arrived. With our hands in our pockets we stood huddled in the gathering gloom, growing colder and wetter by the minute. When at last we got inside, it wasn't much warmer than out. As there was no heating, we lit a coal fire, blowing on the feeble flames to get it going. A couple more people arrived and my induction proper to the local Labour Party began.

First of all the minutes of the previous meeting were read out and were then hotly disputed for the following twenty-five minutes or so. Next we discussed correspondence received by the secretary and there followed a report on what had happened at the constituency management committee meeting. Politics were not mentioned. The occasion remains vivid in my mind because it made a profound impression – it was not quite what I had expected. I was twenty then, in 1967, and the other members all seemed to me somewhere over the age of ninety, although in reality they were probably only in their fifties and sixties. Despite this rather unpromising start, I was persuaded to accompany a couple of members to a City Council meeting. Bit by bit I became hooked, but a career in politics was still not on the agenda.

The idea of becoming a teacher had long been at the back of my mind so, while I was still working to acquire A levels at evening classes, I applied for a place at a number of teacher training colleges. A few replied along the lines of 'Wouldn't you be better off doing music?' or 'Our premises are not suitable for blind people'. Other colleges responded in a more helpful vein, however, suggesting that I should first obtain a university degree since this would enable me to be more readily accepted into the teaching profession.

Following this advice, I applied for a university place, both through the usual forms supplied by UCCA (the Universities and Colleges Central Admissions) and by writing direct to chosen establishments. Manchester University responded that their campus was too scattered to suit my needs, which was probably true.

Following interviews at York and Durham, both offered me a place to read Sociology, which was the 'in' subject at that time. The problem was that I had been away from my mother for so many years and the idea of leaving Sheffield once again did not appeal; nor did I wish to leave Ruth.

In the end Sheffield University offered me a place to read Politics and Modern History. The Politics Department was headed by the renowned and immensely able Professor Bernard Crick. One of the chief courses I was to take, Political Theory and Institutions, would provide an invaluable grounding in philosophical politics as well as in practical, constitutional politics. The opportunity was precisely what I had secretly dreamed of, but never dared believe would come my way.

As may be imagined, I was delighted when Mum read aloud the letter offering me the place at Sheffield. Even she was thrilled. She could hardly believe it: I was the first person in our family to go to university and almost certainly the first within a two-mile radius of our home, so few were the opportunities for people from our background and neighbourhood. We gave each other a hug – then sat down for a nice cup of tea.

It was not love at first sight or, in our case, at first meeting. She was a lively, mischievous and in many ways outrageous blonde with brown eyes and we were planning to go up to university together, but my first reaction, it has to be said, was one of disappointment. She was not what I had had in mind and seemed too petite to be my type. As I came to know her better, however, I succumbed to her charms and we became inseparable. She was very bright, fun to be with, a fast worker and determined to get her own way. Had I been more experienced, I might have handled things better. As it was, life with Ruby turned out to be traumatic.

It had never been my intention to acquire a guide dog. Throughout my teens, from time to time I had come across guide dogs or heard people speaking about them, usually, but not exclusively, in highly sentimental terms. I felt this presented the wrong image, and that a guide dog's work as an aid to independence, dignity and mobility should be of more crucial importance. This was in part due to the fact that, during the sixties, shortage of money had led the Guide Dogs for the Blind Association (GDBA) to raise funds by tugging at the heartstrings of those members of the general public concerned about the plight of the blind. Times have certainly changed, but care over presentation of the case for giving money is still needed. Along with many others, I believe that fundraising, like all other aspects of work concerning guide dogs, should not and must not rely on sympathy. If it does, then the whole point of the work of the Guide Dogs Association in fostering independence is undermined. Guide dogs are not merely cuddly companions. By acting as a pair of eyes to enable a blind person to do a job, or cross a busy street or a crowded railway concourse, a guide dog can take away some of the hurdles involved in getting from A to B, which any sighted person takes for granted.

It was therefore an immense relief when I found that my old school friend Graeme McCreath had trained with a dog which matched my own view of what a guide dog should be. Graeme had a magnificent German Shepherd named Mike. Like all Alsatians (as I was later to discover with my third dog, Offa, who was half Alsatian), Mike was somewhat eccentric, highly strung and over-attentive. Yet his amazing capacity for work, his loyalty and majesty made me think twice and then three times about whether it would be worth training with a dog myself. Finally I decided that, if I were to accept the challenge of a place at Sheffield University and a growing involvement in politics, it would be helpful to be able to move around freely without having to rely on other people or on my own nervous energy and mobility skills. A guide dog would complement my abilities rather than replace them, which would be an enormous advantage over other aids to mobility, such as the old-fashioned white stick or its more modern equivalent, the sonic torch.

In September 1969 at the regional guide dog training centre in Bolton, Lancashire, I was introduced to Ruby, who was to be my companion for the best part of nine years. During a four-week residential training period we would get to know each other and learn to work together as an efficient team. I had not, up to this point, had much contact with the Guide Dogs for the Blind Association, so the learning experience was to be at least as much mine as Ruby's.

Since its foundation in 1931, and even since I first trained with Ruby, the British guide dog movement has grown considerably. In the sixties the GDBA set up its own breeding centre, which is where Ruby was born, and it is now one of the world's largest breeders of working dogs. From a carefully selected breeding stock of 250 Labradors, golden retrievers and Alsatians plus the occasional curly-coat retriever, border collie and the like, approximately 1,000 puppies a year are born. Of these, about eighty per cent will be trained successfully as guide dogs, while the remaining twenty per cent, whose health, temperament or experiences make them in some way unsuited to the specialist task of guiding the blind, will be taken on by HM Customs and Excise, the armed forces, the prison service, the police or perhaps a family.

Until I attended the Bolton training centre, I do not think I had fully appreciated the fact that, while a guide dog's owner clearly has possession of that dog, the GDBA reserves the power to withdraw the animal if something drastic goes wrong or there is evidence of abuse. Throughout their lives, from birth to death, no matter where they may be, the dogs are regularly monitored by the Association. Thus the GDBA is now responsible for a total of approximately 6,500 dogs, comprising the breeding stock plus 1,350 puppies and dogs in training, over 4,000 working dogs and just under 800 who are retired. These are the current figures, but even those applicable when I trained in 1969 were fairly substantial.

Ruby had been training to be a guide dog since she was six weeks old when she was sent to live with a volunteer family, one adult member of whom was designated to be what is known as the 'puppy walker'. With the help of the rest of the family, the puppy walker cared for Ruby and ensured that she became thoroughly adjusted to home life and to meeting new people. Over the following ten months or so Ruby was taught to be clean and to follow the basic commands of 'sit', 'down', 'stay' and 'come'. Like all puppies, Ruby was naturally curious, wanting to investigate everything around her. When she encountered something new, be it a smell, a sound, an object or whatever, she had to learn how to react, whether to 'fight or flight', as it is termed. One of the most important aspects during this initial training is to keep the dog's confidence high so it remains eager to work and open to new experiences.

An unhappy experience can cause irreparable harm and ruin a guide dog's future. I heard of one instance when just days before the handover to the blind owner, the dog was scared when, while passing a butcher's shop, a huge side of beef suddenly dropped in front of the dog. The dog refused to go near the shop again, and its career as a guide dog was over before it had truly begun.

In the hope of avoiding a similar fate, Ruby was walked by at least three different people – her supervisor, her puppy walker and one or more members of the puppy walker's family – in order to teach her to adapt to new situations. She was introduced to as wide a variety of environments as possible, including railway and bus stations, shops, markets and restaurants. She went in cars, lifts, buses and trains, and across bridges, gratings and slippery surfaces, and learned not to fear loud noises, road works and bustling crowds.

Ruby took two kennel breaks at the local training centre to join 'puppy parties'. Held for groups of six, they are designed to accustom puppies to sharing territory and being sociable with other dogs while also preparing them for the second stage of their training, which would be based at the centre. By the end of her stay with her puppy walker, Ruby had acquired the three CS: confidence, concentration and calmness, although in her case the latter quality was rather variable.

It is hard to imagine what a wrench it must be for puppy walkers and their families when the time comes to return the puppy they have cherished to its training centre. I thought Matthew Vanes' account of his experiences as a puppy walker's son, which I came across in the GDBA's journal *Forward*, most enlightening in this respect:

My mother started puppy walking twelve years ago, when I was ten years old, and that is when my dilemma began. I really did believe that all children were told to 'hup up' when crossing a road and were told to 'sit and stay' when entering shops on a shopping expedition. I also suffered the indignity of being told to hurry up and 'go busy' before leaving home!

I became so confused at one point that my parents discovered me asleep on the floor one night and the puppy sprawled out on my bed.

But puppy walkers are cunning people. I thought my mother was being extremely thoughtful when we moved house and she suggested I have the largest bedroom. Not a bit of it, the largest bedroom just happened to be the nearest to the kitchen. Who is first to hear the nocturnal renderings of a lonely, missing-my-brothers-and-sisters, six-week-old puppy? You've got it – the puppy walker's son. Who is it, when the dear little soul is convinced there is a big bogey man hiding in the kitchen, sits on the kitchen floor reassuring it and singing nursery rhymes until it goes to sleep? Yep, that's me, the puppy walker's son.

One would have thought that as I've grown older I would have been able to assert my position within the household. No way! Puppy always manages to get fed, watered and walked before the rest of us get a look in. But now I am experiencing serious, I mean serious, problems. Try bringing a new girl home when there is a six-week-old bundle of fluff sitting in pride of place in front of the fire. There is no competition, man.

Forget it, you've lost again. If only the oohs and aahs were for me! I'm still not sure which is worse, your girlfriend fussing the puppy and ignoring you or, when the 'puppy' has expanded to accommodate its 60LB weight, it tries to squash itself between the two of you on the settee. Cuddling up takes on a whole new meaning.

So I am thinking of setting up a splinter group called the PWO (Puppy Walkers' Offspring) and offering free, yes free, advice to all young people who have suffered in a similar way. Strange though, I always get this funny lump in my throat when my latest rival departs with the supervisor. Perhaps it's the thought of all those sleepless nights to come with the new arrival . . .

At almost twelve months old, Ruby returned to the full-time care of an instructor in the dog supply unit, where she commenced the second stage of her training. Strict obedience was demanded by the handler with plenty of praise and reproof by voice or tugs on her lead. Ruby was taught to ignore any distracting smells and sounds, including other animals and to learn the difference between useful or hazardous features, like kerbs, lamp-posts, bollards and gates. It was instilled in her to walk always in the centre of pavements with a moderate tension on her lead and not to go round corners unless asked to do so. New commands such as 'forward', 'back', 'right' and 'left' were gradually introduced. After a few weeks Ruby started to wear a harness, initially without the guiding handle, and, like all guide dogs, she came to accept the fact that when the harness was on, she was working; when it was off, she could relax.

As training progressed, Ruby was taught how to move round basic obstructions, how to halt on the kerb at the edge of every road and to cross straight over a road when given the command to do so. Once she had mastered the latter, she was also taught that there are occasions when this command should be disobeyed, for instance, when a car is approaching. Despite popular myth, a dog cannot accurately judge the speed of a moving vehicle, so while training teaches a guide dog to stop for a moving vehicle, it remains the owner's responsibility to decide when and how to cross a road. To leave the decision solely to even the most gifted guide dog would be tantamount to asking a two-year-old to cross the M1 on a busy day!

After about six months of learning the basic skills, Ruby was placed with a mobility instructor, Nigel Catterson, for specialised advanced training. While her memory of her previous trainer faded, her confidence was maintained because her surroundings remained the same. With her new instructor Ruby mastered the techniques of judging whether, for example, a gap in a crowd was sufficiently wide for her and her owner to pass through without being jostled, how to sort out who is moving in which direction in a crowd and to find a direct route through, how to stop and start in awkward situations, when to speed up or slow down, and how to avoid complex obstacles.

By all accounts, this had only been the bare bones of Ruby's training, and I was beginning to wonder whether I would ever be equal to such a paragon. My nervous reverie was interrupted by Nigel asserting that careful consideration was always given to matching a dog's character and abilities to the character and lifestyle of its blind handler. The last four weeks of her twelve-week advanced training period had, he said, been spent moulding her to meet my particular needs.

'It seems that all I have to do', I muttered only half in jest, 'is spend the next few weeks learning everything Ruby can teach me.'

How wrong I was. In point of fact the next couple of days were spent with a group of other first-time owners, carrying out exercises designed to familiarise us with the 'feel' of following a guide dog's harness handle, with the instructor playing the part of the dog. This may sound ridiculous and it certainly provided some hilarious moments, but the serious intention behind this role-playing was to enable the instructor to see where any weaknesses in technique occurred on my part and iron them out before Ruby became involved. As I was to discover in later years on return visits to training centres, this role-play is highly relevant to first-time owners, but extremely tiresome for owners who go back for replacement dogs, a fact the GDBA itself is coming to realise. Tailormade courses to suit the needs of individual owners are now being recognised as important, but it has taken a long time to catch up with the kind of choice and personalised approach which has long been a feature of wider social and economic life.

I found the first two or three days with the group rather tedious because everything was done at the pace of the slowest person and we were too often addressed as though we were a bit slow on the uptake, both factors which I gather have changed for the better over the last twenty-five years. The whole residential training course reminded me of boarding school with communal meals and general lack of privacy. It was a trying time for I was eager, though rather nervous, about my imminent start at university. Ruby, meanwhile, turned out to be the fastest dog on the course: the first to retrieve a ball when asked to do so and the first to dive into her bowl of food. I suspected she might turn out to be greedy, as well as bright. It was not long before I began to see her as she really was, without the mystical glow with which all trainers seem to imbue their protégés.

Nigel firmly pointed out to me that an owner's failings can all too easily be passed on to the dog, although this is also, in my view, a good excuse for a dog not having been properly trained or being placed with an inappropriate owner. Nevertheless, without clear instructions, proper control and, when necessary, the strict reinforcement of proper behaviour, a guide dog's performance swiftly deteriorates. Being tough in the early days pays dividends in the long-run. The truth of this advice was later to become achingly apparent as the years with Ruby rolled by. In the meantime, though, our weeks of mobility training went reasonably smoothly. Deftly our instructor encouraged Ruby to transfer her affection and loyalty from him to me, and calmed my anxiety when inexperience led to incorrect handling. Day by day my sense of freedom grew as I learned to be guided by Ruby. It was a tremendously exhilarating experience – I had never before felt so liberated. Secure in the knowledge that Ruby and I would continue to receive on-the-spot guidance and training from an instructor for a couple of weeks after returning to Sheffield, I was eager to go home.

When Mum opened the door to let us in, she was presented with the spectacle on her doorstep of two men and a guide dog all looking highly pleased with themselves. We followed in Indian file as Mum led the way to the front room. As soon as her harness was off, Ruby bounded around the small house investigating her new home – while I went into the kitchen to put the kettle on for a cup of tea.

5

Town and Gown

Total chaos and panic: feathers scattering in the breeze, water splattering into the air, the sound of webbed feet paddling frantically as birds took off right and left. Ruby was up to her usual tricks, chasing the ducks in Weston Park, adjacent to the university. With a sharp woof of delight and paws pounding the ground, she would launch herself bodily into the water in hot pursuit of her quacking victims. She was out of control and thoroughly enjoying herself.

Whenever I think of the three years I spent at Sheffield University, one of the first things which comes to mind is the smell of baking dog. Ruby would be on the window-seat grille above the radiator in my room, drying out after a hectic session at the duck pond. While I listened to tapes or worked at the typewriter, the unmistakable smell of wet dog drifted round the room like a damp mist, permeating everything within reach. Long after Ruby was dry, the smell would linger in the air, a constant reproach for my failure to make her behave properly.

Another aspect of going up to university which remains vivid is the mixture of eager anticipation and acute anxiety which engulfed me during the early weeks of the first term. Students were constantly exhorted to make the most of the opportunity to 'do their own thing', a possibility I found worrying as well as exciting. Knowing that all the other students could see their way around, meet each other and easily make friends left me panic-stricken. Given what I do now, it seems almost unbelievable how excruciatingly shy and gauche I was in those days. Meeting new people, establishing contact and forming working relationships, let alone making friends, seemed impossibly difficult. This doubtless pushed me into my developing relationship with Ruth, who provided a much-needed sense of security.

Ruby, however, shared few of my apprehensions about our new life together; indeed, she took to most of it with the same ebullience she displayed at the pond – like a duck to water. Together we explored the campus and found our way to the university library, only to discover that it contained no facilities for producing material in braille. So we set off in search of the Politics Department. I was thankful to have Ruby with me because the campus contained many potential hazards, not least of which was the Arts Faculty, a superficially palatial modern tower of nineteen storeys. Both sides of the flight of steps leading to the main entrance were flanked by a moat-like structure; if one misjudged the position of the steps, it was all too easy to end up in the water. Once inside the building, we were faced with either a paternoster – a continuously ascending and descending series of lift compartments which one had to leap on and off, of course totally unsuitable for a dog – or with endless queues for the conventional lifts. I decided to take the stairs to the tenth floor, a habit which improved my physical fitness enormously over the coming months. Arriving at last in the correct department, we found Professor Bernard Crick, Head of Politics, and Roydon Harrison, Professor of History, in discussion with a couple of colleagues. While Ruby panted and wagged her tail avidly, I tried to explain the problems of being a blind student.

Roydon Harrison immediately struck me as the archetypal academic, being extremely well read and with an exceptional grasp of history and politics. He left at the end of my first year and became Professor of History at Warwick University, but over the course of time since our first meeting I have come to view him as a reformed revolutionary who nonetheless comprehends the difficulties of practical day-to-day politics and pragmatism. In recent years, he has been on hand with an appropriate recollection, piece of advice or political observation to ensure that values and philosophy are never forgotten. I respect him greatly for that. Although Roydon is now retired, he is still very alert and active, giving lectures in the Far East as well as across Europe, while his wife Pauline is Professor of Biochemistry at Sheffield University. I often enjoy their hospitality – a good meal with a modest helping of political ribbing.

I liked Bernard Crick from the start, although he too left Sheffield in the summer of 1970. His book *In Defence of Politics* set the scene by maintaining that politics is important because it is the only way in which those without wealth and power can exercise any form of influence. I think that political events over recent years have borne out his attack on the cynics of both Right and Left who dismiss political activity as irrelevant, boring or unrewarding, who play entirely into the hands of those who already possess power and to whom democracy is a channel for using government for their own ends. Crick also pointed out a tendency in the sixties for people to become involved in single-issue pressure groups rather than join a political party. Interestingly I think there has been a revival of this tendency in the nineties. I am in no way against pressure groups, but I regard membership of them as complementary to, rather than a substitute for, membership of a political party. All I would ask is: why become involved in a pressure group to pressurise somebody who fundamentally disagrees with you when you can join a political party which is trying to put into power people who do agree with you?

Bernard Crick, as I soon found out, is a mischievous character. On one memorable occasion the professor was found in the Politics Department washroom early one morning by a startled cleaner, who was shocked to note that Bernard was clad only in his underpants. A furore ensued. It transpired that for several months past the eminent Professor of Politics had been sleeping in his tutorial room-cum-office, having, for some obscure reason, been forced to quit the basement flat which until then had been his home. It was not, however, as a result of this little episode that Bernard left Sheffield. He was, he averred, simply fed up with undergraduates – not that this included me, he was quick to emphasise – who, in the revolutionary spirit abroad at the time, did not want to sit exams and claimed the right to determine the content of their courses. The post-graduates at Birkbeck College, London, where he accepted the chair in Politics, were much more to Bernard's taste. We did not lose touch, however, and have remained friends; in 1987 we collaborated in writing a rather rambling but seminal pamphlet, *Socialist Aims and Values*, which was a political and philosophical essay on how Labour might steer a course for the future

between the Scylla and Charybdis of the Militant
Trotskyite Left and the self-serving monetarist policies
of the Tory Right.

To avoid the intrusive sound of my tapping away on
a braille writer taking notes, it was agreed by Bernard,
Roydon and the other lecturers that I could record
lectures on tape, whenever feasible. This decision
proved a boon in several respects. Firstly, so as not to
disturb other students, I was given a study of my own
in which to work. Secondly, listening to the tape as I
transcribed it meant that the content of a lecture sank
in more than it might otherwise have done; it was a
form of instant revision. Thirdly, the tapes were an
invaluable *quid pro quo*: a fellow student who had
missed a lecture could borrow the relevant tape in
return for reading course material to me either out
loud on the spot or on to tape. I hesitated to lend the
tapes too frequently, though, in case everyone decided
to give up attending lectures altogether!

Ruby herself was none too keen on lectures. She did
not like being in places she regarded as boring, that is
ones where she had to lie down quietly in a corner for
an hour or two while I got on with my work. She made
a habit of standing up just before the lecture hour was
over, grunting, yawning loudly, stretching and generally
making it crystal clear she thought it was time to go.
This became such a tradition that it caused student
audiences to break into fits of laughter and the swift
curtailment of many an overlong diatribe by lecturers.
In an article in the *Independent on Sunday* not long ago,
there appeared the following anecdote: 'During lectures
Blunkett's guide dog, Ruby, used to bark every time
Crick mentioned Marx. Crick tried referring to "the
German doctor", but Ruby still barked.' This is an

amusing example of mythmaking. My ever mischievous friend Crick was behind it.

As with higher education countrywide, the quality of our lectures varied hugely. University lecturers had rarely undergone formal teacher training in those days, although they may have been adept at tutorial and research work – but even that was not always the case. Ken Watkins was, however, one of the few members of the department whose lectures were entertaining, illuminating and consequently riveting. He was an ultra Right-winger, who had at one stage espoused Communism and, typical of most converts, he was a zealot concerning his new cause. Outwardly amusing, charming and, more importantly, thought-provoking, deep within he must have been in turmoil, for sadly some years later he was found dead on a railway line. I remember Ken with gratitude.

Apart from a room of my own and being allowed to tape lectures, few other material concessions were made to my disability. I did, however, receive considerable help in other directions. When I first went up to university I was rather shocked to be told that I could not write. To the despair of my tutors, I had never been taught how to present a formal essay, I could not spell and my command of language was below par. Having gently pointed out these deficiencies, a tutor would take me through my essay, attempting to disentangle the points I was trying to make from the impenetrable thicket of tortured prose in which they were hidden. Opaque sentences and phrases were patiently unravelled so that the tutor could form a judgement on and award marks for any perceptive observations and original thoughts we might unearth. In my case quite a lot of my thoughts were pretty 'original' because I had not read many of the books other students had studied. They were also much more widely read in terms of newspapers and journals. Obviously I had a lot of catching up to do.

In addition to helping me improve my written work, tutors also gave me special direction on what was worth reading and even which chapters in a book I should concentrate on. I may have missed out on some material covered by other students, but what I did read was studied intensively and absorbed. Since the main course was entitled Political Theory and Institutions, we were taught practical politics in terms of procedure in the Houses of Parliament and legislative processes, as well as political philosophy, economics and economic history, much of which was very stimulating. One of the most important benefits of university was that it gave me time to read: from Plato and Aristotle, through Rousseau, Mill, Hobbes and the *Leviathan*, to Marx and Alan Bullock. Reading *The Strange Death of Liberal England* by George Dangerfield taught me that books could be entertaining and enjoyable as well as politically enlightening. I began to broaden my horizons and read for pleasure, including poetry, biography and history, encompassing works which were both pleasurable and mentally challenging.

As the weeks passed I really did feel that intellectually my future was opening up, in sharp contrast to my time grinding away at the Gas Board and at evening classes. At last I had the opportunity to revel in books I had never come across before, to develop my own thoughts and test out political beliefs in reasoned debate. I still find it hard to take when politicians and other activists assert a political view without offering any logical argument in justification. Debate is vital. I need to be sure in my own mind that an action or policy is well thought through and sound before I can put it across effectively to someone else. It is worth recalling a vote I won on a Sheffield City Council matter when I outdid my opponent in debate, yet failed to convince him of my argument. I have never forgotten what he said and I struggle hard to ensure that I believe what I say before I try to convince others. It seems to me that one of the problems besetting politics today is that we have lost the art of persuasion through intellectual debate and tend instead merely to indulge in verbal fisticuffs. On television it is particularly apparent when a person does not believe what he or she is saying. This leads to widespread cynicism and to democratic political activity being held in disrepute. The events of recent years have served to reinforce public disillusionment with politics, again playing into the hands of those who do not need representative or participant democratic politics to get their own way. Unfortunately the media's obsession with what is known as the 'sound bite', a fifteen-second extract from a longer interview, contributes to the impression that politicians are superficial.

Not many evenings were spent in typical student fashion on campus. I was living at home with Mum during the first year and so was relatively cut off from university social life. Although I would sometimes stay to participate in a debate, on the whole I treated going to university much like going to the office. My daily routine remained the same. By half past eight in the morning I would be at my study-room desk while fellow students were still in bed. Having had a job, I was accustomed to knuckling down; I took it for granted that a full day's work had to be done. After so many years of evening classes and weekends spent swotting for A levels, continuing to study some evenings and most weekends did not seem unnatural.

Any time left over from university work or Sunday duties as a local Methodist preacher was devoted to local Labour Party politics. During the course of my first year as a student, early in 1970, it became apparent that one of the Labour councillors on Sheffield City Council would not be allowed to stand again for his ward in the forthcoming local elections in May. This was an unusual occurrence in Sheffield politics and was therefore a topic of lively speculation at party meetings in Southey Green. The standing councillor was due to be replaced by Stewart Hastings, a young trade unionist, whose mother I came to know well before she moved to another part of Sheffield. Shortly before the selection meeting at which Stewart was set to be confirmed as the official candidate, he was offered a job in South Wales and a replacement candidate was urgently needed. There was a feeling in the local party that the council needed an injection of young blood and, when it was suggested that I might have a crack at it, I agreed with alacrity. I very much wanted the opportunity to become a councillor.

At the selection conference on 8 February, various members of the committee asked questions including the old chestnut, 'If Mrs Bloggs comes to you and says she's got a blocked drain, what would you do?' to which I replied, 'Well, the one thing I certainly won't do is put my arm down it!' Seriously, though, I then went on to say that being blind would not make any difference. I would simply go along to see her and talk about it, and then ring the public health department to get an inspector along to see it. They appeared satisfied. The combination of my evident commitment and enthusiasm, allied to the consensus in the local party that it was time for a breath of fresh air, seemed to swing the branch's decision in my favour. They made a brave choice — selecting a man who was only twenty-two years old, and blind, to stand for a safe seat. It was a risk because there was no way of knowing for certain that I could do the job. It was a gesture of confidence I hope I repaid over the eighteen years during which I represented the ward. The other two Labour candidates for the ward were councillors of long standing with proven track records. One of them, Winifred Golding, who had served on the council for many years, became my mentor, providing invaluable help and support.

Normally in very safe seats such as the one I was standing for, the local party scarcely lifted a finger to canvass new votes. Knowing this, one of the first questions I asked was why we were not delivering a leaflet to the small section of the ward which was owner occupied. 'They'll vote Tory,' came the reply. My response was that I was not surprised they voted Tory if we never did anything to change their minds, never delivered leaflets, never knocked on their doors. I felt very strongly about this because it was symptomatic of the attitude within the Labour Party in those days which eventually contributed to the Labour Government's demise in 1979. Within the local party, as within similar groups all over the country, it was not widely recognised that the world was changing rapidly around us. The ward for which I was standing was ninety-five per cent council housing, and, together with the neighbouring ward, made up a housing estate said to be the largest in Europe; the remaining five per cent of houses were privately owned. I took the line that we should not believe any section of voters was lost to us. Instead our message to owner occupiers ought to be: 'Your interests are our interests, your concerns are our concerns. The fact that you bought your home is neither here nor there — it doesn't change you, it doesn't change us.' I would emphasise the fact that I lived in the neighbourhood and would fight for what residents needed in terms of improvements to education, social services, libraries, local transport and such like, while also speaking out on wider political issues.

When I first expounded the view that we must target Tory voters, I did not realise I had inadvertently put my finger on the fact that the Labour Party was at a watershed: unless we attracted a broader spectrum of voters, we were finished, or soon would be. This became a constant refrain of mine over the years that followed.

In the meantime I had to get out and practise what I preached. This was my first experience of canvassing and it was to prove much more trying than I had anticipated, despite the fact that I was on home territory, in my own neighbourhood. Nowadays somebody always comes along with me, but canvassing for that first election in 1970 I only had Ruby for company. Stuart Lowe, a generous fellow student who frequently read university course material to me, used to drive Ruby and me round the streets with a loudspeaker on the car roof, trying to persuade people to come to public meetings and to turn out to vote on election day. Stuart was a very personable young man, diffident, but totally committed. Rather like me, Stuart was not someone who was enjoying the lighter side of life, so we relished some fairly intense political discussions as we whizzed round the ward in his battered Mini, me in the front passenger seat with Ruby posing majestically in the back. Having dropped us off at the spot where we were to canvass, Stuart and the Mini would disappear noisily up the street leaving a trail of exhaust fumes in their wake.

'Find the gate,' I would say to Ruby. Having done so, she was instructed to 'find the door'. Having knocked on the door, I would then extend my hand towards the person who opened it and introduce myself. Sometimes my outstretched hand met with the face of a child, no doubt often dangerously close to the eyes. On other occasions a piping voice might respond to my greeting and I would ask in dulcet tones, 'Is your Mum or Dad in?' only to discover that the person I was addressing was a youthful parent. Canvassing provided so many opportunities for making a fool of myself that I really had to steel myself to continue. Sometimes I would even berate myself out loud: 'Well, if I'm asking other people to trudge the streets delivering leaflets, knocking on doors and collecting subscriptions on a purely voluntary basis for no other reason than that I want to be elected and they believe in what we're fighting for, then I cannot, must not, let them down.' The combination of personal ambition and the desire not to disappoint my supporters proved an effective stimulus, constantly driving me on.

By the end of every hour-and-a-half stint of canvassing, we were both drained by nervous exhaustion. In the end Ruby became almost psychotic. For days after the canvassing was over, whenever I took her out, she would drag me through any gateway we came to, intent on the task of finding the front door. After a while, of course, she realised this was no longer what was required of her and life returned to normal, although she remained reluctant to get into Stuart's Mini.

There was, however, an unlikely sequel to our canvassing experiences. Almost a year later, one Sunday night, there was a loud knocking at the front door. With Ruby beside me, I answered it. On the doorstep I found a police officer, who presented his identification and introduced himself as Superintendent Jones. He sounded very stern.

'Step in, won't you?' I asked and led the way through to the sitting room. 'What's the matter? What can I do for you?' I assumed he must have called to see me in connection with a council matter.

'I'm sorry to trouble you,' he said, 'but I've been asked to come to see you on a serious matter. Do you drive a Mini?'

'Of course I don't,' I replied somewhat sharply, 'you must realise I'm blind.'

'That's the significance of my enquiry,' responded Superintendent Jones, audibly drawing himself up to his full height. 'It has been alleged that you were seen driving round the Ecclesfield district of Sheffield.'

'Oh, really,' said I, 'and I suppose my guide dog Ruby was sitting in the front seat next to me navigating?'

'No, sir. According to my information, the guide dog was behind you in the back seat.'

The corners of my mouth twitched and, in an effort not to laugh out loud, I said, 'Superintendent, it's absolutely ridiculous. When did you receive this allegation?'

'Yesterday, sir.'

'And do you know what date it was yesterday?' I asked.

'Um, er, I don't understand what you mean, sir.'

'Superintendent, it was April the first – April Fools' Day.'

Almost imperceptibly the superintendent shifted the weight on his feet. 'Well, I don't think that's very funny, sir,' he said almost accusingly. 'It's a serious allegation.'

'And I don't think it's very funny you asking me, a blind man, whether I have been driving a Mini round Ecclesfield with a guide dog in the back seat,' I retorted, at last exasperated by the man's lack of humour. There was a momentary silence.

'I think perhaps we'd better drop the matter,' said the superintendent at last, evidently down, but not out. 'I hope I never have occasion to ask you again about such allegations.'

'So do I, Superintendent,' I responded rather too loudly as I closed the front door behind him, 'so do I.'

Some years later, having regaled a small group with an account of this farcical episode, someone asked if I had heard about the newspaper report that the police had stopped a man in America for dangerous driving and discovered that he was almost blind. In the seat next to the driver was what the Americans call a seeing-eye dog. When asked in court how he managed to cope with level crossings, traffic lights, other vehicles and such like without crashing, the driver was reported to have replied that the dog barked in a variety of keys depending on what kind of obstacle they were approaching. When I heard this, my second thought was: Good Lord, perhaps Superintendent Jones was not so stupid after all.

While Ruth's parents expressed some displeasure and concern when we got engaged, I do not believe they seriously tried to dissuade her. My mother, on the other hand, was most decidedly against it and said so. As with most young people, the more forcefully she tried to dissuade me, the more determined I became. The more she urged me not to rush into such a major commitment, the more I felt she was clinging to me and that I must disentangle myself. She advised me to see the relationship in perspective over the long-term and to wait to find out what life might hold in store for us. I realise now that she was very wise, but nothing she said at that time could make me change my mind. I was determined not to spend the rest of my life at home with my mother.

Both Ruth and I felt that marriage was the appropriate next step in our relationship. The support we had given each other in the course of countless days and evenings spent studying and working together had engendered a mutual sense of security and dependence. At least she takes an interest in me, I thought, which was not a good reason for getting married, but many people settle for companionship. Only when they later find love do they realise that they were not in love before.

I proposed to Ruth one day when we were standing in front of Sheffield Cathedral, a rather unlikely spot for a romantic to choose. In July 1970 we exchanged vows at the Methodist church near our homes. Mike Newton was my best man and I had a double whisky before setting out for the church. After the reception Ruth and I went for the weekend to York and then on to Ireland for ten days. Our honeymoon was not a success and got off to a bad start. My eating onion soup for dinner on the first night may not have helped. One of my most abiding memories is an encounter with some travelling people in the main square in Galway. They were raising money by taking turns to lie on a bed of nails while

someone stood on their chest. This incident remained
with me and seemed a portent of things to come.

We took a coach tour via Blackwater, Connemara,
where I duly kissed the Blarney Stone, and to the island
of Valentia, which was approached by boat since it was
not then attached to the mainland by a bridge. At some
point we hired a couple of bicycles and I fell off mine,
unfortunately landing in a very prickly bush. At the
seaside Ruth declined to venture into the water but I
longed for a swim. I waded into the sea up to my thighs
at which point I panicked: I thought I had lost the use
of my legs. The sea was ice cold. The *coup de grâce* was
a place called Ballybunnion, which was bally awful.
One day I would like to return to Ireland and give its
undoubted charms a second chance.

6

A RUBY BEYOND PRICE?

'SORRY, SIR, BUT you can't take the dog inside. They're not allowed in the Palace of Westminster.'

I was in London with a group of fellow politics students from Sheffield on a field course which involved visiting government departments and listening to debates in the House of Commons. Ruby and I had finally reached the head of the queue for the Visitors' Gallery, snaking its way along the pavement towards the arch of St Stephen's entrance to the Houses of Parliament. One of the burly policemen on duty at the bottom of the broad flight of steps leading into the building stood resolutely barring our path. Ruby sniffed him apprehensively.

'No, sir,' said the policeman, firmly, when I explained how vital it was that Ruby accompany me, 'I'm afraid she'll have to stay here with us.'

'I don't think that's a very good idea,' I replied with some feeling. 'She's much better when she's with me and under control.'

Pleading proved useless, however. Rules were rules and had to be enforced. There were two consequences to this decision, both of which were predictable. Firstly, Ruby was led reluctantly to the police cubbyhole beside the entrance steps, where, as soon as I had departed, she made her displeasure evident by spending a penny on the floor — not something any of my subsequent dogs would have done, but completely in character with her propensity to protest. Secondly, equally typically, I made a fuss.

Between us we interested various newspapers, including the *Daily Mirror* and the *Guardian*, both of which ran stories under the headline 'Guide Dog Refused Entry to Palace of Westminster'. The line taken was that Ruby and I had been denied our democratic rights. Further publicity, this time in a lighter vein was generated by a

hitherto college rules permitted cats on the premises but banned dogs. The whole question generated a memorable exchange of correspondence on the letters' page in *The Times* by eminent professors and academics, who vied energetically with each other in putting forward abstruse linguistic arguments for and against the notion of dogs being regarded as cats, all conducted in an atmosphere of mock seriousness and immense philosophical ingenuity. It was a classic exchange.

In the end so much publicity was generated and so much pressure brought to bear that the authorities were forced to relent. Thus it came about, in due course, that Ruby made history by being the first dog to set paw within the hallowed portals of the Palace of Westminster. This was only a partial victory, however, since access to the Visitors' Gallery remained forbidden to guide dogs for a long time to come.

David in the driving seat

I wish I'd taken one piece of toffee instead of two

David shows an early love of dogs – or is it Cognac?

Arthur and
Doris Blunkett

Am I in safe hands?

Homesick at
Rowton Castle

Best foot
forward
with Ruby

With the
Lord Mayor,
Peter Jackson

In the thick of
training with
Teddy at the
Guide Dogs
Training
Centre, 1978

The Queen's
visit to Sheffield,
1986

Celebrating
with friends,
Joan Barton and
Peter Price, on
being elected
MP for Sheffield
Brightside, 1987

With Offa,
Central Lobby,
House of
Commons

Visiting
Laurie Lee at
Littlecourt,
Slad, 1991

Down Memory
Lane with Offa
at Rowton
Castle, 1994

FA Cup Final 1993, with my sons, Alastair,
Andrew and Hugh, on the way to watch
Sheffield Wednesday v Arsenal

Celebrating with Valda as
Sheffield Wednesday win
the Rumbelows' Cup

Give me your answer, do!

Happy Birthday, Dad. Hughie has made a cake

In at the Deep End!

Following our frustrating first visit to the Houses of Parliament, later that same day Ruby and I rejoined our fellow students to pay a visit to the then newly formed Department of Trade and Industry. Rather astonishingly, given that nowadays it is difficult even for a parliamentary delegation to gain access to a minister, we students had been granted a session with Peter Walker. He had recently been appointed Secretary of State for Trade and Industry by Prime Minister Edward Heath, following the Conservatives' General Election victory in 1970.

As we seated ourselves round a large conference table, tea and coffee were brought in and the meeting got under way. Walker began by outlining the workings of his department and his policy aims. After about twenty minutes or so, when he was well into his stride, the room suddenly began to reverberate to the sound of loud snoring. Astonished, he stopped in mid-sentence, leaned forward in his chair at the head of the table and scanned the faces around him. Another volley of snores rang out.

'What's that?' asked Walker in a startled voice. He could obviously see we were all wide awake.

'I'm very sorry, Secretary of State,' I confessed, 'it's my dog.'

'Your dog? What dog? Where?'

'Beneath the table. It's my guide dog, Ruby,' I replied as apologetically as I could without sounding ingratiating, while attempting to nudge Ruby into silence with my foot.

'Oh, well, yes, I see,' said Walker, evidently relieved. 'That's all right. I'm sorry – that's fine. Hello, Ruby, where are you then?' He patted her, she thumped her tail on the floor and the meeting resumed.

On the train home to Sheffield at the end of the course, anecdotes were swapped about the trip and there were chuckles over Ruby's antics. Gradually, as the others dozed off, the compartment fell silent. I mused as I stroked Ruby's head, which was resting on my knee, while she snuffled in contentment. The first of what I hoped would be many visits to Westminster had not gone quite as smoothly as I had expected. Over the years, Ruby came to regret the decision to incorporate her in the political arena. Long hours of what were, to her, endlessly boring Sheffield City Council meetings and debates as well as meetings held nationally on matters relating to local government lay in store.

On occasion, Ruby would fall asleep from sheer exhaustion rather than from boredom. In the course of an average weekday we must have walked tens of miles, travelling back and forth between home, university and the Town Hall. After setting out early from home to put in an hour or two of study in my room in the Arts tower, there would be two or three lectures or seminars starting at nine or ten o'clock, and then I would head into the centre of the city around lunchtime. Here at the Town Hall, I would read correspondence, sort out problems with colleagues and check the times of meetings before returning to university for any after-noon seminars and lectures. In the late afternoon, it was back to the Town Hall once more for council or committee meetings and then on to local Labour Party meetings before heading for home to try to finish some university or ward work before bed and oblivion.

At that time there was no provision for either office space or secretarial help for ward councillors, so all notes of meetings, research or briefing information and correspondence concerning my constituents had to be dealt with in my room at the university or during spare moments at home. There were not too many of the latter, since on Sundays I was often still acting as a local preacher or involved in some other form of church activity.

The combined workload of university and council matters was an onerous one. Not surprisingly, most members of the university Politics Department thought I was crazy to take on so much, and many of the staff expressed concern that I would blow my chances of a good degree by devoting such a substantial amount of time to the council and my ward. After the departure of Crick and Harrison, my main memories are of working with Pat Seyd and Stuart Walkland. Pat was a young lecturer from Portsmouth, heavily committed to Labour and particularly illuminating on the Party's role in modern British politics. Stuart, my tutor, on the other hand, was a pink Conservative who had flirted with the Liberal Party and was the author of *The Parliamentary Process*, an important work well regarded at the time. A pleasant-natured man, he used me as a Labour Party benchmark during discussions and seminars. 'David,' he would say, turning towards me, 'what does the Labour Party think about this?' To which I would reply, 'Well, I really don't have a clue, but my view is . . . ' and then explain my ideas.

Both Pat and Stuart were very supportive, unlike one lecturer who often marked down my papers or essays when they concerned local government. He did so, he said, because what I had written did not accord with his own experiences in Nottinghamshire twenty years earlier. Interested and surprised by his attitude, I naturally disputed the case. Sheffield was in the process of major reorganisation and there had been a number of significant changes over the intervening twenty-year period. Yet, as far as I can recall, he remained unmoved by my arguments and continued to give me a hard time.

Equally unexpected, perhaps, was the way I was viewed by the majority of my fellow students, given the supposedly liberal atmosphere of the late sixties and early seventies. A large number were Right wing, including Philip Norton, now Professor of Politics at Hull University and then a dour, dedicated Young Conservative, who always spoke out on behalf of the Conservative Party. The most active and vocal politics students, though, were at the opposite end of the political spectrum, voicing support for the views of the university Socialist Society, reflecting aspects of the revolutionary Left, the International Marxist Group and Socialist Worker. Most of them thought I was weird. Being a member of the Labour Party was considered deeply reactionary by the ultra Left and they regarded my involvement in local government as a peculiar and reprehensible diversion from theoretical politics. They seemed to feel I was soiling my hands by actually practising politics on local housing estates as opposed to devoting myself solely to reading Marx, discussing Hobbes or exploring the libertarian ideas of Mill. Such divergent attitudes led to many a heated debate, which I enjoyed immensely. It was life and soul to me. In addition, groups of us joined most major political marches and demonstrations including one at Old Trafford against the Springboks' tour and a number of marches in London, like the one against the Industrial Relations Act in 1972, said to be among the largest in history. Ruby preferred rallies to some of our more sedentary pursuits.

Fortunately I had friends who, with Ruth, used to read material on to tape for me. Most of them, like Stuart Lowe and Alex Erwin, were on the same course as me, though one or two were taking joint courses, like Lesley Chapman who was reading Politics and Japanese, and I tried to get them to read works which were relevant to their own studies as well. George Guest, a postgraduate student, volunteered to organise the circle and devise a rota. The support and encouragement I received from these friends and helpers were invaluable. Eventually too I had the help of Lorraine Simpson, a young mother of two children, who was willing to do brailling for me. In addition she offered to take over much of the reading on to tape hitherto valiantly undertaken by Ruth.

At this stage Ruth was busy doing a teacher training course, having been discouraged by the teachers at her school from applying to university. Much later I discovered that Ruth had mixed feelings about the amount of time she had spent reading for me: in part she had welcomed it as a contribution to our relationship, but part of her resented the large amount of time involved. While I valued her help, I would never have wanted her to help me out of a sense of duty which would later turn to resentment. For my part, I genuinely did my best to encourage Ruth to develop her own talents and abilities, and I believe that in no small measure I helped increase her self-confidence, although neither of us would claim to have had good social skills – something it certainly took me, personally, a long time to remedy.

We were lucky enough to start married life with a home of our own: a terraced house near the university. When we purchased it in 1970, it was extraordinarily cheap and turned out to be a sound investment. Within four years the value increased threefold as house prices everywhere rose swiftly and our area in particular became more fashionable. Ruth's father was a dedicated do-it-yourself enthusiast and in the first two or three years the house rang to the sounds of continual renovation work. The structure was certainly in need of substantial repair, which was presumably why the original purchase price was so modest. Even when I was swotting for final exams, there was the constant sound of work in progress. I found this both irritating and distracting, and I was not as grateful as I might have been for my father-in-law's generous endeavours. On the other hand having a home of our own did provide a sense of security and I appreciated the space it afforded to be by myself. Sometimes on a Sunday evening, listening to work tapes, I used to fall asleep, and when I awoke, I would have to listen to the tape all over again.

Setting up home is a testing time for any young couple while they learn to live together, and Ruth and I were no exception, but it did not take us long to realise fully how incompatible we were. We certainly did not see eye to eye on tidiness and housework, and this caused some friction. I am by nature a tidy person because knowing where things are is crucial for any blind person to be able to keep on top of things.

I have heard it said that people become politicians in order to compensate for the lack of satisfaction in their private lives. This may well be true in some cases. Those enjoying a loving and fulfilled home life are hardly likely to want to attend tedious meetings night after night, which is how most people get into politics. Certainly some senior politicians and successful go-getters are fundamentally unhappy people, and looking back I realise I was too.

Despite the best endeavours of Ruth and myself, our marriage was never a success in terms of our relationship. All my energy and commitment therefore became increasingly channelled into university studies in the short-term and political activity in the longer term. Politics became a substitute for a contented marriage, although I did not recognise this until years later.

I cannot speak for Ruth, who may well have felt the same, but I lived in constant hope that things would eventually improve. The reason I persevered was that I believed our difficulties could be overcome if we put sufficient effort into it. Of course, some relationships do evolve in this fashion but, looking back, I realise I was naive and immature to believe ours could. Our mistake lay in not recognising that the relationship was never going to work at a point when it might have been feasible to extricate ourselves. Instead, over the course of time, we accommodated each other in an almost platonic but stormy relationship which we survived for seventeen years. I think perhaps both of us believed that, without each other, the only alternative would be loneliness, and that we were better off sticking together than striking out on our own.

If we had had a less restricted social life with more opportunities for relaxation, perhaps we might have learned to be more at ease with each other. As it was, there did not seem to be much time to spare for having fun. The circle of students who read for me were the friends I knew best and they tried to involve me in the lighter side of student life, but I disliked late-night parties. I felt very ill at ease amid the din of loud music, when I could neither see what was going on nor hear who I was talking to. At the few parties I did go to, people tended to be lying about on floor cushions or sprawled on beanbags, where I tripped over them. I infinitely preferred spending time with friends who invited us to their home for supper; a heated discussion would almost inevitably ensue across the dining or kitchen table but, despite vehement disagreements, the evening would end amicably. Not all friends were associated with the university, however; some I met through church, such as Mike Newton, and his wife Pat. Mike and I originally came across each other at a conference concerning overseas development organised by the church, at which, as was my wont, I made a speech. One of my least endearing features as a young man was that I could never shut up; wherever I went, I felt an irresistible urge to leap to my feet and give forth. Nevertheless Mike and Pat came over to me at the end of the conference to introduce themselves and we became friends.

There is no point in dwelling with regret on the youth one might have had. I made choices, for better or worse, and placed politics at the core of my life. When I first became a councillor, my aim was to improve radically the lives of the people I represented. I genuinely believed that by serving on the council I could improve their lot: housing, environment, education, transport and suchlike. To some extent it was possible in the early seventies to effect real improvements, as was made evident by the achievements of my mentor, Councillor Winifred Golding. She fought for donkey's years for a new library, and won. She battled hard to have more public lavatories built, and won. Some may dismiss these as trivial achievements, but they did improve people's lives, and Winifred could take pride in countless such modest victories. I wanted to do the same, to witness life around me improving and to feel that I had made a real contribution. I still feel the same today, although my scope is broader. Besides my wider aspirations, one of my early priorities for my ward was to clean up the local environment. This included cleaning up and making safe a very large derelict air-raid shelter, and the transformation of a hazardous refuse-strewn field into a usable play area for children. These and other issues were pushed through with the help and backing of Labour colleagues, chief among whom was, of course, Winifred. Throughout the election period and my first year or so as a City Councillor, Winifred continued to offer crucial advice. Even when she resigned her seat as councillor after successfully being elected alderman just two months after I myself had joined the council, her support remained unwavering as she encouraged me and generally kept a motherly eye on my progress.

The leader of Sheffield City Council in 1970 was Ron Ironmonger, who was, in my view, one of the most outstanding traditional council leaders of the day. Later knighted for his services to local government, he was a man of tremendous integrity. By seven o'clock each morning he would be at his office desk in a local factory before moving on to the Town Hall to spend the larger part of the day and evening sorting out council matters. Totally committed to public service and public provision, in a very tough, no-nonsense manner he gave me key lessons during my early years on how our council should be run and how to conduct myself. His chief strength was that he was prepared to involve everyone in decision-making and he encouraged opponents to listen to each other's views. On occasion, though, he could be extremely tough and put someone down with a few

terse words. From him I learned that the art of leadership is not simply knowing how to lead, but that it is
important to set aims and argue for what you believe in
– and also to accept defeat with dignity.

Alderman Sidney Dyson was a totally different kettle
of fish. He was an old-guard political fixer. There was
nothing he liked more than to stitch up deals behind the
scenes, generally in the Town Hall members' quiet
room, where he would recline in an armchair, his
protuberant paunch reverberating in time to his *sotto
voce* mutterings. Alderman Dyson could easily have been
a character in a novel by J B Priestley.

The day came when it was his turn to take over as
Lord Mayor and I was invited to move the vote on
behalf of the City Council. Given our mutual antipathy,
I was an unlikely choice, but the idea was mooted by a
likeable old warhorse by the name of Isidore Lewis,
who was Chairman of Finance and Deputy Leader.
Isidore had witnessed an unfortunate episode when I
had collapsed from dizziness while addressing members
in the council chamber. He felt the sole effective means
of restoring my self-confidence was to give me the
opportunity to make a high-profile public speech as
soon as possible. He proposed that I, as the youngest
member of the council, should move the vote for the
installation of Sidney Dyson as Lord Mayor, knowing
full well that he was the last person on God's earth who
would ever have agreed with a brash Left-winger like
me. It was a bit of mischievousness on Isidore's part, but
an opportunity for me, so I agreed to do it.

On the momentous day the chamber was packed
to the gunnels with officials and civic dignitaries in
their finery and regalia – in every way it was a most
prestigious gathering. I stood up to speak.

'Lord Mayor, Lady Mayoress, ladies and gentlemen, I cannot think of anyone who could more amply fill the Lord Mayor's chair than Alderman Sidney Dyson.' I paused almost imperceptibly to allow those present to ponder the literal truth of this statement, as we faced the substantial form of Sidney Dyson squeezed on to the seat of the mayoral throne.

At that very moment events took a dramatic turn. Ruby made a sudden dash for freedom from beneath my seat, where she had been reclining, and took off round the council chamber at high speed. With ears flapping and tail swishing from side to side with excitement, she made two full circuits of the room before coming to rest with a painful-sounding thud on the stomach of the new Lord Mayor. There was an explosion of laughter from the assembly, while an outraged Sidney Dyson attempted to remove Ruby from his lap.

After retrieving Ruby and securing her lead, I apologised and continued with my speech, which became slightly more fulsome than it might otherwise have been. I expounded upon the matchless service Sidney had given, outlined some of his achievements and, while admitting that he and I had often had our differences, I suggested that his election as Lord Mayor was a worthy recognition of the contribution he had made to the city. Dyson forgave me, my reputation as a speaker was redeemed and from that day on my life in politics went from strength to strength. Ruby was never again permitted an opportunity to let me down in the council chamber; thereafter her lead was always kept firmly wrapped round my leg.

Nothing, though, could restrain her once she was off the harness in an open space. I will long remember

Sunday afternoons when, walking alone, I would let her go for a romp and she would refuse to come back. Ruby was in a number of respects unsuited to her role as a guide dog, but her refusal to return when called was the most infuriating. Seeing me standing alone in the midst of the park, pleading forlornly for her to return, passersby would say, 'She's just sniffing round a bush about fifty yards away,' and then they would add, 'She's seen you – she's running away in the opposite direction.' If there was water near by, she would head for it and go for a swim, and she particularly loved the small reservoir near our home. When at last she did finally condescend to return, she would inevitably come right up to me before shaking herself furiously, so that we both went home completely drenched.

Even in the supposedly post-revolutionary period of the early seventies, graduation day, when degrees were conferred in a rather grand and formal ceremony at Sheffield Town Hall, was still widely regarded as a major event. For my mother it was a dream come true, a day to savour. Her son had at last gained a degree, which she hoped would open doors to the kind of life she had witnessed in her younger days when she had shared a household in the rich south-west of Sheffield. Now that her lad had his foot on the first rung of the ladder, it seemed to her that he might aspire to such heights. To say she was looking forward to the degree ceremony with bated breath would be an understatement. The day was very nearly ruined, however, by Ruby.

Swathed in my freshly pressed gown and feeling exceedingly nervous, I followed Ruby up the steps on to the platform and approached the Chancellor of Sheffield University, Rab Butler, to receive my degree certificate. (Rab Butler, a leading Conservative thinker, was later squeezed out of the premiership by the Conservative Right.) Had I been accompanied by any of my later guide dogs, this would have been a relatively easy exercise, although in the case of Offa there was a fair chance he would have whisked me so fast from one side of the platform to the other that I would have passed the Chancellor in a blur. Being Ruby there was a different hazard. With a will of her own, she took me squarely to the centre of the stage and then sharp left down to the footlights. She wanted to enjoy her moment of glory. There was a vast audience and loud applause – for Ruby this meant taking a bow. With only inches to spare, the Chancellor caught me by the sleeve, thus preventing me from toppling over the edge and probably breaking a leg. The situation was redeemed and Mum's heart returned to its normal pace. At the end of the ceremony we were able to emerge intact and in high spirits into the sunshine outside the Town Hall, where we mingled in the throng of celebrating graduates surrounded by congratulatory friends and relations. Ruby remained confidently aloof and unabashed.

7

JUNGLE MANOEUVRES

'BRICKLAYERS I' WAS to prove the acid test of 1973.

In the summer of 1972 I had graduated from university with a 2:1 in spite of the forebodings of the lecturers who had warned that I might not get such a good degree. When the results were posted, I have to confess that I myself wondered whether I might have achieved a first had it not been for my heavy involvement in local politics. Nevertheless I was delighted and relieved. A respectable degree meant that the goal of a career in teaching was nearer to becoming a reality.

After I graduated, I went on to do a one-year post-graduate course leading to a teaching certificate in further education at Hollybank College in Huddersfield. When I was first elected to the council, I was not eligible for an allowance because I was not losing income from a full-time job by carrying out my council duties. I had a grant, and fortunately by this stage Ruth had qualified as a geography teacher and had obtained a post at Sharrow Lane Junior School in Sheffield.

For me one of the most interesting aspects of my course was a stint of teaching practice at a further education college in Sheffield. At my insistence the permanent staff of college lecturers had been told to treat me as they would any other student teacher, but many of them were sceptical about whether a blind person could teach effectively, and were full of doubt about how I would cope. In the event I was given a spread of courses to teach, including a class known as 'Bricklayers 1', which was for first-year students of bricklaying on day release from building sites.

To these lads the idea of general/liberal studies was an open invitation to rebellion. As I entered the classroom for the first time I could sense that this group was going to be a challenge – a contest of Henry Cooper proportions – blind or not, they were determined to do me down. I was nervous to the point where my stomach literally knotted up. Every week it was to be the same.

'Get out your paper and pens, please.'

'We left them in the other room,' would come the reply.

I had to make a judgement whether or not this was true. 'Stop messing about,' I would respond in my best Kenneth Williams voice. Raising a laugh was crucial to get them to do what I wanted. 'I want you to make notes on some slides I'm going to show you,' I might say. 'Please pull down the blinds.'

'They're down already,' came the instant response.

'Oh, so you've been sitting here in the dark, have you?' That would get them going. 'You lot would drive over your own grandmothers given half a chance,' – and they agreed!

Gradually we would begin to do some work, but then I would hear disturbances, such as paper darts hitting somebody, or worse. It was unfortunate that the class had to be held in a spare science laboratory, where the students sat on high stools at workbenches supplied with water and gas. Not a good idea. An outbreak of coughing and choking would be accompanied by the dread smell of gas. Once that had been switched off, someone else would start spraying water round the room.

'What on earth are you doing with that tap?'

'I'm washing me hair,' came the unlikely reply.

'What do you mean – washing your hair?'

'Jack's put chewing gum in me hair,' a mournful voice replied.

Every session with Bricklayers 1 was a battle. A minor breakthrough occurred, however, when one day I took into class a cutting from the *Sunday Times* about an aircraft which had crashed in the Andes; most of the stranded survivors had eventually resorted to eating the bodies of their dead companions and there had been a lot of media coverage. I pointed out the moral and physical dilemmas inherent in the situation, and asked the class for their views. At first they reacted along the predictable lines of 'What's wrong with eating a nice bit of brain then?' But slowly I pulled them round to talking sensibly about this moral maze – what they would do, how they might feel – in order to get them to imagine the awful reality of such a situation. It was a struggle to sensitise them and persuade them to address the issues, but it was interesting and rewarding.

At the end of each class I would stagger back to the staff room and slump exhausted into a chair.

'Are you still wanting to be a teacher?' demanded a couple of lecturers.

'Just,' I gasped.

'Well done! That class has finished off quite a few student teachers.'

It gave me great satisfaction to prove to the doubting

Thomases that I could indeed manage to control a class and even perhaps teach them a thing or two. The experience was an ordeal but at the time I knew I had to get through it and not admit defeat. Compared with teaching practice, which I think Ruby enjoyed more than I did, the rest of the training course was easy. Educational psychology and the history of education were especially useful and stimulating.

Swapping views on the course and teaching practice with Bob Glendenning as we drove back and forth between Sheffield and Huddersfield was an enormous help. On rainy days, though, the trip was a bit of a nightmare as his old car leaked like a sieve. Water would be slopping about the floor to such an extent that sometimes we passengers had to sit with our feet in the air to avoid having to spend the rest of the day squelching around in sodden shoes.

One evening on our way back to Sheffield from Hollybank College, my companions decided to drop in at a house shared by a group of student friends. We were lounging about, mulling over the state of the world, when I sensed that Ruby was becoming uneasy. She began to sniff and whine and despite my efforts she refused to settle.

'What on earth are you doing?' I asked one of the others. 'I can't get her to be quiet.'

At this, one of them explained that they were dishing out marijuana and asked if I wanted to share a joint. I declined. I never felt the need to try drugs. Daily life seemed challenging enough without getting stoned. Being a pedigree Labrador, a breed frequently trained to be sniffer dogs, Ruby was driven to complete distraction by the scent of marijuana. All we could do was retreat as speedily as possible to the relative fresh air of Bob's old banger. Although I often felt I was missing out on a lot of the fun fellow students seemed to be enjoying at both university and training college, the drug scene never appealed.

In any case, there were council meetings to attend and work to be done. While Ruby lay on the carpet, licking her chops as she dreamed of foraging in dustbins for her favourite junk food, a working party of councillors including myself spent a large part of 1972 into 1973 arguing about the policies to be included in a draft manifesto for the inception of the new South Yorkshire Metropolitan County Council (SYMCC). Major changes were afoot.

Bob's leaky car was not the sole form of transport which preyed on my mind. One of the main motives behind becoming a councillor had been to implement a policy which I have wanted for a long time: to provide free or, at the very least, affordable public transport in and around Sheffield. This aim was also one of the chief reasons behind the formation of the new SYMCC. Within the working party, a core of about four of us drafted a transport policy regarded by many, particularly Right-wingers and those outside the area, as revolutionary. It was certainly innovative. Even within the Labour Group there was dissension, but when the time came, our proposed policy was accepted at the party manifesto meeting in Rotherham. It was all systems go. Thus, in canvassing for the SYMCC elections held in May 1973, the main thrust of our local Labour Party manifesto was the introduction of our cheap fares, integrated transport policy for the area, the most interesting features of which I will endeavour to outline as succinctly as possible, since public transport is still the subject of widespread concern in the nineties.

The aim of the policy was to subsidise local transport so that buses and local trains were sufficiently inexpensive, frequent and reliable to persuade those who had cars to leave them at home, and to enable those who did not to be more mobile without having to spend too much of their wages travelling to work, going shopping, enjoying leisure pursuits or visiting relatives. We proposed introducing a flat-fare rate for journeys within a six-mile radius of the city centre. It was free to travel in Sheffield city centre itself, while elsewhere journeys were free for pensioners, 2p per child and 10p per adult – the cheapest fares in Britain, pegged in 1974 and frozen until 1986. Research showed that, not only was car ownership lower in South Yorkshire than in the country as a whole, but also, in common with the rest of Britain, of the few families who did own a car, in the vast majority of cases it was the man who took the car to work, leaving wife, children and any other dependants without private transport. Thus, whether or not a family owned a car, they benefited from cheap public transport. There were environmental spin-offs too in the sense that the better the public transport, the less the need for expensive road building, the fewer the car parks required and the lower the level of pollution from exhaust fumes. It was demonstrable also that the more people who travelled by bus or train, the more the council could afford to maintain and expand the transport service to meet their needs: the more passengers there are, the greater the income and the lower the fares.

At the manifesto stage we could not prove every detail of this on paper, although later, in practice, it turned out to be the case. The electorate was offered a new transport system, which would cost less and meet their present needs and more, all of which could be provided through a transport subsidy generated from rates income.

Thus, when Labour won the local elections that May, our innovative transport policy had considerable popular support, and I continued not only to represent my ward as a city councillor but also, *de facto*, became a member of the newly created South Yorkshire Metropolitan County Council. In addition, shortly afterwards, I gained a fresh and more influential platform for my views by being elected to serve as a member of the Executive and Policy Committee of both councils. These local cabinets had executive powers to formulate council policy, primarily in terms of dealing with finance and personnel resources. They could also act on behalf of their respective councils when the councils were not meeting. It was a heady prospect.

The most urgent target in my sights was the preservation of our transport policy. Apart from leisure activities and some dabbling in the arts, transport was fundamentally the *raison d'être* of the SYMCC and it came to be the subject of continual dispute over the following twelve years. Almost immediately a number of council officers, including my old friend Ron Ironmonger, raised objections to the policy on the grounds that neither council could afford it, it had never been tried before and public transport ought not to be subsidised at the proposed level. So we put Labour's manifesto to a council vote after changing the word 'Labour' to 'council', and it was passed. We then turned to the officers and said, 'You've got to work to this now, because it's no longer part of a Labour Party manifesto, it is now council policy.' We did this both with Sheffield City Council and with the SYMCC.

The choice of who was to be the first leader of the SYMCC was between the former leader of the West Riding County Council and the Leader of Sheffield City Council, Ron Ironmonger. After considerable jockeying, Ron won and he proved highly adept at steering the council during its tricky early years. Despite having argued strongly against acceptance of the new transport policy, he accepted defeat gracefully and did everything in his power to see that the policy was implemented efficiently. Observing his demeanour in such an awkward situation was a lesson I have never forgotten. He was close to my heart. Later on Ron suffered a stroke and I well remember the day when I visited him in an old people's home. Although he had difficulty speaking properly, and therefore holding a coherent conversation was not easy, he very obviously valued having someone talk to him about the past. He could still understand perfectly well, but the fact that he was no longer his former articulate self was most distressing. Later his son Duncan was for a short time Deputy Leader of Sheffield City Council, which would surely have delighted Ron, but sadly he had to retire from the Council after serious heart surgery

In the meantime our transport policy began to take effect and, in fact, we kept it going for twelve years. During this period there were two major hiccups. The first occurred in 1975, when the Labour Government – Lord forgive them – intervened in the person of William Rogers, who was then Transport Minister, but later defected to the SDP. He declared, in effect, that it was not Government policy to allow any council to use money as it wished in order to subsidise transport. He announced that the Government would withdraw the transport supplementary grant, which had been made available on a formula to all local authorities as part of the Government's overall contribution to transport costs. This was a serious blow – we lost £9 million, an enormous sum at the time. There was a huge row within the Labour Group, the leadership, although in favour of the policy, urging us not to go against the Government. Some of the officers threatened that if we stuck to our guns it might be *ultra vires* (outside the law). In the end the motion to maintain our transport policy was passed by a majority of three votes. Fortunately our actions turned out not to be *ultra vires*. As a delegate for my constituency I attended the next Labour Party Conference, where I publicly defended our actions in the face of Government criticism expressed by Shirley Williams, who, as a prominent member of the National Executive Committee, had been given the task of replying to my points in a debate. I have always had a lot of time for Shirley, despite her eventual defection to the SDP. She is very bright, but I am afraid she had not got a clue about transport and the Conference overwhelmingly voted in favour of the SYMCC's policy. How could they not? It was not 'mere Socialism', as claimed by detractors. It was sound common sense.

The second crisis was brought about by the Greater London Council (GLC) adopting our policy in 1982 and launching it under the slogan 'Fares Fair'. Naturally, because it affected the capital, the policy received an enormous amount of publicity, generating untold controversy, until finally its legality was challenged in court by Bromley Borough Council, who won on the grounds that the introduction of the policy had not been technically correct. The officers of the SYMCC, in turn, urged capitulation but, as Leader of Sheffield City Council, I took legal advice on the position. The lawyers' view was that the judgement regarding the GLC did not apply to the six metropolitan county councils then in existence.

We passed on this advice to Merseyside County Council, who were embroiled in a legal dispute begun by one of the major city stores. Their policy was not in fact on full throttle because they had followed in our footsteps only two or three years before this crisis blew up, but in turn Lord Justice Woolf ruled that they could carry on. As it transpired, the SYMCC continued its subsidised transport policy right up to the point in 1986 when, along with the GLC, the metropolitan county council was abolished by the Conservative Government. Nicholas Ridley, Secretary of State for Transport, introduced deregulation outside London, which led to a free-for-all in terms of tendering for contracts to run transport networks. In addition, the Tories introduced rate capping of council budgets, including transport, to the point where it became impossible to carry on. However, Sheffield City Council continued to subsidise public transport for a further year until we were finally forced to admit defeat and abandon the policy.

South Yorkshire's local public transport policy continues to be the subject of nostalgia in Sheffield, where the city centre has become choked with buses since deregulation. Indeed, a decade later, the Government have now accepted our argument lock, stock and barrel with their proposed subsidies in relation to the privatisation of the railways. I still regard it as one of the most important achievements of my political career to date and, in the light of current developments, the subject is far from dead.

It may easily be imagined how enthralled Ruby was by the numerous meetings involved in formulating and enacting these council policies. On the other hand, she did enjoy travelling, more than I did anyway, and there were countless bus journeys as we beetled back and forth between home, the City Council offices in Sheffield, Barnsley College of Technology, where I started work as a junior lecturer in September 1973, and the SYMCC headquarters, thankfully also in Barnsley. It was a hectic round, in which we seemed to be hopping on and off trains or buses all the time.

One day, as Ruby and I stepped off a bus in Sheffield and set off down the road, I heard a small child squeal, followed by an outburst of laughter from the crowd at the bus stop where we had just alighted. I was momentarily nonplussed at this unexpected merriment, but went on my way, wondering if perhaps they were laughing at me for some reason. It was not until some six or seven years later that I discovered the truth. During one of my weekly constituency surgeries, a pleasant elderly woman came to see me and, in the course of conversation, she looked at my guide dog and remarked that it was not the same one I had had before.

'No,' I responded, 'this is Teddy. The guide dog you must be thinking of was Ruby, a Golden Labrador.'

'Yes,' she said, 'she was lovely looking, but very naughty. I remember one time when I was standing at the bus stop, you and Ruby got off. As she passed a toddler eating an ice-cream cornet, Ruby swiped the cone right out of the kiddie's hand, without a moment's hesitation. There one minute, gone the next. We could all see you had no idea what she'd done. The little kiddie's face was a picture. We had to laugh. You went off down the road blithe as can be. I cried laughing. Fancy a guide dog doing that, eh?'

I was mortified, but this was only one of many instances of Ruby's greed. One of the disadvantages of Labradors as guide dogs is that they are by nature like vacuum cleaners where food is concerned. Unless trained otherwise, they can scavenge without the owner knowing. Ruby's ability to steal food while on the harness became legendary. All too frequently, as I later found out, people were too polite to let me know what she was doing. During a camping holiday near Bridlington friends informed me she had eaten their bacon and eggs straight out of the frying pan. As for the tea trolleys which constantly circulated the council offices and Barnsley Technical College, the trays of cakes and iced buns on their lower shelves were seldom safe from Ruby's depredations. Nothing was. If she were off the lead anywhere in the vicinity of a dustbin, she would be in there like a shot, head down inside, rooting in the depths for scraps, while her bottom and tail waggled obscenely in the air. Such forays had most insalubrious consequences for her tummy and waste matter, as well as for the reputation of the GDBA. No dog of mine was ever again allowed to behave in like manner, though I had to ask myself how much of the blame was mine for allowing misbehaviour during Ruby's crucial first months with me at home.

Ruby far preferred the hours we spent at Barnsley Tech' to those endured in council departments, and I think the students, once they became accustomed to the situation, were quite pleased to see her. Certainly I found tutoring the combination of politics, industrial relations, economics and economic history a fulfilling challenge. At first I had to be careful which students I asked to help with the overhead slide projector or to write on the blackboard. It became easier, however, once my appointment was confirmed and fixed classes were allocated to me. Then, in the course of a couple of weeks, I could build a rapport with the students and, with their participation, create an atmosphere in which we could all work towards the same goals. During the first couple of years I encountered the same problems as any new teacher. Finding time to prepare lessons was extremely difficult.

However, lack of sleep for this reason was soon overtaken by lack of sleep from feeding a baby, with the birth of my first son, Alastair, in whom I found great joy. He was born on Sunday morning 27 March 1977 and I well remember returning home from the hospital to an empty house to make myself some breakfast of bacon and eggs. I overcooked them, but they tasted wonderful. In fact everything seemed marvellous. I was immensely proud of Alastair and used to take him in a pannier strapped to my chest for walks through the woods, even in the most dreadful weather. No wonder he put on weight quickly – he had to to survive! I loved him dearly. He would clamber out of his cot and I would wake to find him wrapped in his eiderdown at the bottom of the bed, trying to crawl under the bedclothes for a cuddle.

When Alastair was a toddler of two or three with a wonderful mop of soft, blond hair, I would sometimes take him with me to work at the council offices and even into meetings. In those days it was unusual for a father to take his child to work and, in retrospect, it must have been extremely irritating to many, but as there were no crèches at the time, there was sometimes no alternative. Fortunately my own staff were very tolerant. In spite of taking him with me whenever I could, I do regret not being able to spend more time with Alastair, particularly in his early years while I was juggling three jobs.

With a reduction of only four hours in my teaching commitments at Barnsley Tech' plus considerable time spent preparing for classes and marking essays, and the workload at both Sheffield Town Hall and the SYMCC's Barnsley headquarters, a reassessment of my commitments was inevitable. A modicum of rationalisation was called for and, to this end, I decided not to stand for re-election to the SYMCC's Executive and Policy Committee in the May following Alastair's birth. In the event, however, the free time which might have resulted from this decision was devoted instead to chairing Sheffield City Council's Family and Community Services Committee (Social Services), a position to which I had been elected in May 1976. This was a job I relished, and I soon got my teeth into it.

As a youth visiting my grandfather in the geriatric ward, I had vowed that, if ever the opportunity arose, I would endeavour to lift people out of such appalling surroundings and conditions. Now, among other things, I had the chance to do precisely that. One of the first initiatives I took was to set about changing the rules and reorganising services in order to remove elderly people from what were virtually workhouse conditions. I put pressure on the local health authority to close the Fir Vale hospital geriatric unit and other similar units, and in their stead we built homes, run by the local authority, for the elderly and those who were mentally or physically infirm; they were clean, pleasant places. Other improvements included the expansion of the home-help service, which was increased by ten per cent in one year alone. Although I would have liked to have achieved more in this respect, I did feel that the changes initiated went some way towards fulfilling the promise I had once made.

I was also concerned about a four-legged geriatric. By now, Ruby had reached the ripe old age of ten and had developed a limp. Greatly worried, I contacted the GDBA, who examined her and found that she had arthritis. It was time for her to retire as soon as a suitable replacement could be found. In the meantime, Ruby and I continued with our daily round much as usual. One afternoon, we alighted from a bus and, after pausing at the bus stop so that I could slip the harness on her, we set off down the road. To my dismay it became instantly evident that Ruby could scarcely walk: she was staggering along at a snail's pace. Oh God, I thought, her legs have given out completely. As we made our way towards a pedestrian crossing, a man who was passing exclaimed, 'Your dog looks in a bad way.' There was no choice. 'I'm going to have to carry her home,' I replied, trying not to let my voice quaver with emotion. As I bent down and slid my hands round Ruby to lift her up, I was aghast to discover that the main strap of the harness, instead of being across her chest, was between her front legs, holding her so tightly that she could move no more than a few inches at a time. What a relief!

It was clear, nevertheless, that Ruby's working days were drawing to a close, for on mornings when the rain poured down or snow splattered against the windowpanes, she would creep away to hide behind the television rather than stand wagging her tail eagerly by the front door, waiting for her harness to be put on. Retirement could not come soon enough for her.

Fortunately, because Ruth was at home much of the time with Alastair, we were able to keep Ruby with us.

Once she realised she no longer had to work, the arthritis was much improved. She resumed all her old habits of escaping over the garden wall and burrowing in dustbins, scavenging scraps until she blew up into a barrel shape. When my new guide dog Teddy arrived home with me, Ruby behaved like a grumpy old lady, barking at the interloper and seeing him off whenever he dared approach his mat which was next to her basket. This despite the fact that Teddy was much larger than she and in fact too big to fit in a basket. She was thoroughly tetchy towards him, until she found that he was out with me most of the time, and then she relented somewhat.

Sunday mornings used to be my time off and at half past eleven or twelve I would set off to walk through the woods of Grenoside and up on to the ridge overlooking the Pennines and the upper Don valley, which runs west towards Manchester. Sometimes I went alone, but there were usually family, friends and dogs to keep me company. During the years of Ruby's retirement, there would be the new guide dog, Teddy, young, strong and vibrant, racing ahead and, beside me, Ruby, gradually growing smaller as age took its toll. One bounding about with half a tree branch in his mouth and the other trotting along, sniffing all the way until eventually she became too infirm to enjoy those scents which had always made her life worth living. Our destination was the Cow and Calf pub, which in those days served a hand-pumped Sam Smith's real ale. I have never been a beer drinker, preferring wine, but an occasional real ale is also a pleasure. With a children's room and a pleasant garden, it was my sort of pub. Ruby especially enjoyed this country haven and when she finally succumbed at the age of sixteen, I was deeply saddened by her death.

For months afterwards golden hairs clung tenaciously to clothes and soft furnishings. Although she may not always have been loyal and reliable, and would certainly have won no medals as guide dog of the year, she had affectionately given me considerable service. We had been through some difficult and testing times together – not all of them Ruby's fault!

8

TOUGH TIMES WITH TEDDY

MEETING TEDDY WAS an amazing experience. The sheer size of him compared to Ruby warmed my heart. Here was a dog whose body was so far off the ground that I was bound to feel if he were trying to pick scraps off the pavement or his movements indicated that he had become distracted. Here was a dog – a chocolate-coloured, curly coat retriever/Labrador cross – who needed brushing, but did not shed golden hairs all over the carpet, furniture and my trousers. Here was a dog who appeared not to be obsessed with food and took a genuine interest in where I wanted to go. My sort of dog. He was big and magnificent, and also extremely fast. Immediately we began training together I started to lose weight. Later it was to cross my mind that the hernia which had to be repaired in 1980 might have had something to do with Teddy's strength and the muscle power required in dealing with him.

I had learned the lessons of the previous ten years and was careful to ensure that I followed the rules by imposing maximum discipline tempered by affection and praise. My return to Bolton Guide Dog Centre in 1978 to train with Teddy was different in some respects from my previous visit. Firstly I had more confidence and knew what I was doing. Secondly I was extremely busy and believed that three weeks (the GDBA were not pushing me to stay the full month) out of a hectic schedule would be grossly inconvenient. I took plenty of work with me and, in fact, found time to write a complete treatise on Labour's inner city policy, which was in part a response to a speech by Peter Shore two years earlier and to his subsequent actions as Secretary of State for the Environment. These were the days when not only did I think I knew it all, I was sure that I did!

There were, as I discovered, a number of people on the course who had tragic backgrounds. Among them was a young man from Nottingham, Tommy, who was superb at engineering. He could put a car engine together by touch and yet had no hope of obtaining a job in his chosen field. In order to ensure that boredom did not engulf him, every minor task of the day, from shaving to making a cup of coffee, had been made to last for as long as possible. Now, he was over the moon at the prospect of being given a guide dog and evidently loved the one allotted him. Having been 'imprisoned' in his own room, with only his family at home for company for so long, the dog would provide the first taste of freedom since he had lost his sight. It was wonderful to witness and proved a salutary experience for me, who took getting around, being accepted and doing all the normal things in life completely for granted. Tommy was so grateful and enthusiastic that it made me feel humbled.

Other aspects of my second stay at Bolton were not so warming. The institutional atmosphere had not changed sufficiently to be liberating and encouraging of independence. Far too often blind adults are treated as though they are still children and, although enormous progress has been made over the last twenty years, a residue of this still existed in the late seventies. The facilities to enable people to get their own breakfast or to make telephone calls from their bedrooms are instances where change is now rapidly taking place, but which were lacking then.

Training with Teddy, whom I nicknamed 'the gentle giant', under the eagle eye of trainer Steve Wright, was physically exhausting and emotionally rewarding in fairly equal parts. Another trainer, Peter Smith, whose wife had been involved in the early training of Teddy, told me some years later how one day he and his wife, who was five months pregnant at the time, had taken Teddy out for a run in the park. Upon recall, Teddy had raced towards them at such a powerful speed that Pete, fearing his wife might be knocked to the ground, leapt in front of her and took the precaution of turning his back on him. Scarcely had Pete done so, when he was almost thrown flat on his face as an enthusiastic Teddy wrapped himself like a shawl round Pete's shoulders. He said Teddy was the only guide dog he knew who obeyed recall at shoulder height. An avid listener to the *Goon Show* on radio, Pete affectionately coined the adjective 'goony' to summarise certain aspects of Teddy's character. It suited him well.

When we returned together to Sheffield, I was constantly astonished by Teddy's willingness to work and his dedication to getting the job done: looking out for my needs rather than his own, plodding along when the going was easy and searching out the best ways when it was difficult. One of the few minor drawbacks to Teddy was that, because of his size, it was not easy to squeeze him into small spaces. He was deft at curling up compactly beneath seats in buses, but fitting under desks was sometimes tricky – although he usually succeeded in the end.

With his tight curly coat, I was thankful to discover that Teddy never moulted, providing he received a daily grooming. However, like Ruby, he did have a sensitive stomach. In the weeks following our return to Sheffield, Teddy steadily lost weight, which I feared was due to the relentless nature of my schedule as a lecturer, councillor and Chairman of Social Services. In conjunction with Steve Wright and the GDBA, after considerable trial and error, we eventually fathomed that Teddy's regular diet of Pal and Winalot simply did not suit him. Just in time we switched him to a composite feed called Febo, to which water was added. All did not immediately return to normal, however. While his weight and strength returned, Teddy developed a strange reaction to his new diet: his teeth began to rot. Awful visions of a toothless guide dog haunted my dreams, but swift action was taken to remedy this and Teddy returned to full health. This was a stressful phase, not only because I was seriously concerned for his welfare but also because, with my guide dog off-colour, the pressure of work became infinitely harder to support. However, within a matter of weeks, Teddy was back on form and fighting fit.

In 1978 the sitting MP for the Penistone Constituency, John Mendelson, died following a long illness. As a result, a by-election was called in what was a safe Labour seat, but it was a far-flung, semi-rural constituency which spanned the boundaries of both Sheffield and Barnsley. The contest for the Labour nomination was strongly fought and I put my name into the hat. In the event I lost the selection by a single vote, which was a salutary experience and one which I have never regretted as it gave me the opportunity to mature, to learn and to start living a little before entering the portals of Westminster.

Despite my disappointment, I offered to help in the campaign along with everyone else and was asked to speak at a public meeting as the back-up to the main draw of the night, Denis Healey, the Chancellor of the Exchequer at the time. My job was to keep the meeting going while Denis drove up from London. An easy task you might think for me – but my speech went on, and on, and on, as we waited for Denis to arrive. After about forty-five minutes, believe it or not, I started to run out of ideas and was growing desperate. When I openly confessed to the audience that I sincerely hoped Denis would be with us very shortly, a deep voice just to my right, unmistakably that of Denis himself, said, 'I've been here for twenty minutes, young man, but keep going – I am enjoying it.' Momentarily flustered, I sat down, firmly resolving that if ever a similar situation arose in the future, I would make sure someone gave me a nudge when the next speaker arrived.

Meanwhile, Teddy and I both needed substantial reserves of energy to cope with the weight of meetings, travel and responsibilities of my dual career. I was still a full-time lecturer at Barnsley Technical College and continued to be an active ward councillor. The latter entailed not only holding regular surgeries, at which constituents could visit me to discuss problems, but also generated a large amount of correspondence from inhabitants of the ward. Many hours were spent at my typewriter, responding to constituents and firing off letters on their behalf to relevant departments and officials. How there was time to do all this, I am not sure.

On the other hand, I was fortunate in that invaluable help was available in dealing with correspondence generated by my chairmanship of the Social Services Committee as it was the custom for the secretary to the Director of Social Services to assist in dealing with the Chairman's paperwork too. At that time Lynn Brown was in the post and she was very pleasant, as well as efficient, and my load was lightened significantly by being able to dictate letters to her.

At that time the City Council met monthly and so too did the main committees and sub-committees. This meant that I attended on average three council meetings of one form or another per week. In addition I had to attend meetings of organisations such as trusts, environmental groups and school governing bodies, one of which I chaired. There were local Party, ward and constituency meetings to attend also. When I say my life comprised endless meetings, I mean precisely that.

If in rare moments of tiredness and frustration I paused to wonder what I might be missing as the lighter side of life in the Swinging Sixties and Seventies passed me by, the thought did not linger long. There seemed little point pondering what might have been or envying those contemporaries who led more carefree lives. I was far too serious and politically motivated to dwell on such matters. On the contrary, I recognised how fortunate I was to have become a councillor at such an early age. It had allowed me to rise unusually swiftly, for those days, to the position of a committee chairman. In the seventies, particularly outside London, it was common for councillors to wait a decade or more for such promotion, whereas I had achieved it within six years. When the turnover of councillors became much faster during the eighties, people expected to be given a committee chairmanship within two or three years. Teddy took it all in his stride.

Our first winter together, 1978-9, was a very bitter one, with snow lying deep on the ground for long periods of time. One morning, when the usual lift from Bob Glendenning was not forthcoming because he was marooned at home in Derbyshire, Teddy and I made our laborious way to Barnsley Tech' via three buses and a five-mile walk. Upon arrival, cold and exhausted, I found that only a handful of staff and students had managed to turn up. Within an hour or so, by lunchtime, it was clear that unless we began to head for home with some speed, we would not get home at all that day.

Heading downhill from the college to the railway station to try my luck by train, I ran into a fellow city councillor, Clive Betts. (Many years later, in 1987, he was to take over from me as Leader of Sheffield City Council and is now MP for Sheffield Attercliffe.) He too worked in Barnsley and was making his way home as everything closed down around us. Warming our hands at an ancient stove in the draughty waiting room at the station, we were relieved when at last a train crawled in beside the platform. Promptly we scrambled aboard and, in jovial mood, settled down for the journey home.

Through the snowy landscape the train proceeded slowly until at last it ground to a halt. Anxiously we waited to see what would happen; the station where we were due to alight was nowhere in sight. Then the message came through that our train would stay where it was for the foreseeable future. Apparently, three earlier trains were already lined up in front of us at some frozen points. What happened next was quite bizarre. In order to get off the train I had to jump down six feet from the compartment over the line and down a steep, snow-covered embankment. Teddy, rather wisely, refused to jump into this white abyss, so I leapt forth alone. By the time I reached the bottom of the embankment I was thoroughly soaked and fed up. By dint of much coaxing, Teddy was persuaded to join me. Once Clive and I parted company, Teddy's presence was to prove crucial. The 'gentle giant' literally hauled me through the snow that icy winter's afternoon as I followed in his footprints up miles of totally deserted, snowbound streets to our home in Grenoside on the hill north of Sheffield. Whereas I had no clue where pavements ended and roads began, Teddy was sure-footed, strong and determined. Without him, I might well not have got home safely that day.

Within ten years of becoming a ward councillor, in May 1980, shortly before my thirty-third birthday, I was elected Leader of Sheffield City Council and in the following July was appointed Chairman of the Association of Metropolitan Authorities Social Services Committee. It was a period of elation and excitement, as I looked forward to introducing many innovations and improvements. As though to cap it all, a second son arrived on the scene on 13 July. As with Alastair and later Andrew, the birth occurred on a Sunday, a strange coincidence. Hugh Sanders – the latter name after my grandfather, Sanders Blunkett – was a bright, inquisitive infant who is growing into a charming young man, but with a tendency, like his father, to think he knows it all! As with his elder brother, he learned early to endure the rigours of outdoor life. Within a month of his arrival, we set off for a holiday in Scotland with near neighbours Helen and Keith Jackson, and friend Clive Betts.

Helen, at the time a Sheffield City Councillor, went on to become MP for Sheffield Hillsborough, while Keith, then Vice-Principal of the Northern College, is now head of Fircroft Adult Education College in Birmingham. He and I co-authored the book *Democracy in Crisis: The Town Halls Respond*, published in 1987, which catalogues not only the struggle between local and central government throughout the eighties but also the innovative economic and social policies carried through by Sheffield City Council, which were in turn reflected in the activities of local authorities elsewhere.

Desperate to rediscover the glories of Scotland, we rashly discounted the fact that it was not the ideal place for a late summer holiday. A solitary croft perched on the edge of a loch in an extremely wet, windy August, with midges biting furiously, was not the best location for a newborn baby. To keep warm, Hugh spent most of the time snugly tucked up in his carrycot beside a radiator in the main bedroom.

One lunchtime, on an especially dreary day, someone had the bright idea that we should drive to the nearest pub for a wee dram and a bit of cheer. A couple of miles along the road, with Teddy breathing down my neck from the back of the car, a thought suddenly struck me. 'Where's Hughie?' I asked the others. And where was he? He was still tucked up in his cot back at the croft where we had left him. What guilt as we sped back to retrieve him! He has, of course, been quite unforgettable ever since.

Back home in Sheffield once more I realised that, if I were ever to spend any reasonable amount of time with Alastair and Hugh, a rationalisation of my workload was called for. I was juggling the equivalent of three jobs and only succeeding in doing so by the skin of my teeth, which was not good enough. I wanted to devote the majority of my time to fulfilling the role of leader of the council, so my lecturing commitments had to go. After negotiations with Barnsley Education Authority, it was agreed that I go on secondment for a three-year period, at which point their legal liability to contribute to my pension would terminate. In return I agreed to repay all my councillor's allowances. At the end of the day it meant that I received a basic living wage, albeit less than when I had been lecturing full-time. In effect Barnsley Education Authority treated me as though I had been elected Lord Mayor of Sheffield rather than Leader. Teddy and I no longer had to make the tedious journey from Sheffield to Barnsley, which led to a surprising difference in our energy levels and allowed me to concentrate on politics.

When I took over the leadership of the City Council from my predecessor, George Wilson, I was fortunate to inherit his personal assistant, Valda Waterfield. Over the years since we first met, she and her husband Trevor have become close friends. Valda has continued to work for me since I became a Member of Parliament and now runs my constituency office in Sheffield, but our working relationship did not get off to a good start. While George Wilson had employed Valda part-time and had left her to deal with his correspondence, I wanted her to work full-time, including some evenings. I also preferred to answer my own correspondence and was pedantically methodical in terms of administration. My first act was to leave her a typed list of what I expected her to do, including a suggestion that she increase her hours. Looking back, I realise this was a crass thing to do. What I should have done was sit down with her to discuss what I wanted and how it might best be achieved. Why she did not walk out on the spot remains a mystery, though she has told me since that it was a very close call! Instead she set about helping me implement a very different set-up from the one she had known before. Gradually, we built an excellent working relationship, which has continued over the years. Later, we were joined by Jean Marples, another caring member of staff who shares our drive for hard work and efficiency, tempered by a sense of humour, which helps to keep us sane.

One of the key factors which saved my bacon so far as retaining Valda's services and, thereby, her breath of sanity was Teddy. She would often take him out literally for 'a run' while I was tied up in meetings. Teddy never walked. His legs were so long he always seemed to canter and Valda was pulled along behind. This did not pose too much of a problem except in winter when the pavements were icy and it was rather like making the journey on skis. In summer, when time permitted, I would join Valda for a much-needed brisk walk to a wide green area in the city centre, where Teddy could run and where it was possible to sit and enjoy a sandwich lunch in relative tranquillity, putting the world to rights, away from the telephone.

I am afraid I had a reputation for being extremely strong-willed and bumptious, and my election as Leader had therefore realised the worst fears of some senior staff at the Town Hall, despite the fact that I was not the Far Left candidate for the job. They anticipated that I would make their lives a misery, which in the event I do not believe I did, but I was very tough on what I wanted to do and was perhaps in some instances over the top in expecting people to jump into action. I made it transparently clear that I would not accept incompetence and that I expected chief officers to run their departments with the utmost efficiency. This obsession with efficiency was for me allied to a strong sense of public service and I did feel that in some quarters around the country the old-fashioned paternalism, which I dislike, was being replaced by something even worse – a seeming indifference to the needs and aspirations of the very people we were employed to serve.

'Hard Left' was a label commonly employed by the media with regard to me and my fellow Labour Councillors during the seven years I was Leader of Sheffield. For our part, we preferred to describe ourselves as 'Firm Left' (as opposed to 'Soft Left', which would have implied that we were malleable under pressure): durable and reliable, without being inflexible. We aimed to steer a different route from, on the one hand, the old Labour tradition of paternalistic 'do as I say' politics, in which everything was determined by the Town Hall and, on the other hand, Militant Tendency, which was rampant on Merseyside in the eighties. We endeavoured to create socialist policies which would be credible, viable alternatives to those of the Right of the Conservative Party as exemplified by Margaret Thatcher's monetarist deregulated market economics.

Ever since the days when I first canvassed votes in my ward I had been keen to inform and involve as many residents of Sheffield and its environs as possible in the aims and decision-making of the City Council. We tried to give people a greater say in their community and make them feel that the services belonged to them, not to the council. In our attempts to open up council policy to popular influence, we not only continued to hold regular ward surgeries but also increased the number of public meetings in order to air key issues, such as developments in our cheap-fares, integrated transport policy.

Since canvassing, holding surgeries and standing on a soapbox at meetings inevitably had a limited impact, we tried other, more effective means of communicating with local people. The local BBC radio station was already well established by this time, and I soon learned how vital both radio and television were as means of reaching the broadest possible audience in a short time. The electorate became better informed than was ever before possible, and as a bonus I discovered I enjoyed broadcasting to what I hoped was a captive audience.

Under strong television studio lights my eyes have a tendency to flicker; it is a reflex action, which cannot be remedied. Every now and then someone suggests that I wear dark glasses. Dark glasses, a thick white stick and a stoop may be the image that some people have of blind people, but it is certainly not one I am prepared to accept. Take me as I am or leave me has always been my attitude to life and remains so today.

In the course of numerous visits to the studios I came to know Michael Green, now head of Radio 4, who was very encouraging to a broadcasting novice like myself and an enterprising programme maker. It was illuminating working with him. Many years later, when I became an MP and had to spend much of my time in London, I discovered that it is not so much what you know as who you know that seems to count as regards career advancement. This is an attitude with which I am not at ease, never having been a great one for networking. At the end of the day, true friends, of whom there are inevitably but a few, are those who stay in contact and are supportive through bad times as well as good. It irks when someone appears out of the woodwork only when success is in the air.

During my time as leader of the council, we did in fact initiate neighbourhood committees of tenants on council estates, providing them with environmental budgets to enable them to make decisions concerning their own patches. Long before it became common-place, we were keen on local people serving as governors and managers of schools and colleges. Among other innovations, we also encouraged disabled and elderly people to become involved in the running of the day centres they attended.

It has to be admitted that we did not altogether succeed. Perhaps if we had moved faster and pushed harder to implement these innovations, there might have been more lasting fundamental changes. As it was, I think we only began to scratch the surface of persuad-ing the general public to feel that the schools, libraries, transport, health and social services, were theirs and not the council's. Another factor which hampered our efforts was that the changes met resistance from a number of officials and councillors who were frightened of allowing control of services to slip out of their grasp. They regarded the services with which they were connected as personal fiefdoms.

Despite having the best possible motives, wholehearted success also eluded us with regard to our economic endeavours. For instance, we set up a Department of Employment and Economic Development, which I still believe was correct in concept, but we under-estimated the enormity of the task of drawing in those with expertise in commercial enterprise. We recognised that Britain was working within a global economy and that the market economy was dominant, whether we liked it or not. We therefore tried to develop a middle course between old-fashioned command-planning economics, which we realised would fail, and laissez faire Thatcherite economics. BBC Television broadcast a schools programme concerning our 'Middle Way' policy in Sheffield. At one stage we sincerely did believe that we had found an effective alternative to Thatcherism: a decentralised municipal socialism which would provide a catalyst, drawing together business, commerce, trade unions, community groups and workers to save the declining steel and engineering industries. Funds were invested by us to help draw up alternative plans, but in the end we had to face the fact that even our investment in public services could not compensate for what was happening to our industrial base. The world was changing rapidly. Over 50,000 jobs were lost in Sheffield steel, engineering and associated industries between 1981 and 1984. The social, as well as economic consequences, were traumatic. Friendships, sense of belonging and community, pride in work and status among workmates, and simple political or friendly socialising all disappeared as factories stood idle or were bulldozed. On the Council, all we could do was to try to maintain the social fabric by investing in services, giving people confidence and pride in their city, and bolstering their morale and belief in the future.

The enormity of the market forces unleashed by global economics was underestimated by most indus-trialists, entrepreneurs and politicians alike, who were still thinking in regional or, at most, national terms. The global tide swept all their smaller spheres sideways.

Britain is only just beginning to emerge from the impact of that inundation, with a seriously depleted industrial base. This is why education – including lifelong learning, superhighways for information technology and the university for industry – is so vital if Britain is ever to compete with the countries of the Pacific Rim. There were prophets who warned of this: regarded as being on the Far Right, they called themselves Futurists. I read their articles and recall a television series on their theories entitled *The New Enlightenment*. At the time their ideas were viewed as a threat to be blocked, whereas in fact they offered the challenge we needed to take up.

In 1982 I met with Mike Ward who chaired the Greater London Enterprise Board. Together we decided to initiate a joint research project on the future of cable and interactive communications. This resulted in a joint Sheffield–GLC report which was launched nationwide, spelling out the importance of fibre optics and the cabling of Britain. That was over fourteen years ago. It is now a key element in Labour's policy for the future, but had our recommendations been implemented at the time, Britain would by now be a world leader. Some you win, some you lose.

Sheffield was unusual in that I believe we managed to be radical without the lunacy which affected some Labour councils. We were certainly distinct from Militant Tendency, which advocated old-style dictatorial politics, where voluntary organisations were *persona non grata* and decisions were made centrally and applied no matter what the local people wanted. We in Sheffield kept the support of the electorate even when we inevitably made mistakes. Any politician who claims never to have made a mistake has never taken leadership or attempted to implement radical ideas or move in new directions; it is very easy to be a cabbage.

Being leader of a controversial council inevitably gave me a higher national profile than the position would normally have warranted. Barbara Maxwell, then producer of BBC Television's *Question Time*, thought it might be interesting to invite a brash young northern Labour leader to join the panel. I was naturally flattered to be asked since in 1982 it was rare for any politician below the rank of a minister to be included. The prospect of making my first appearance on national television before an audience of millions made me nervous, so I was determined to be thoroughly prepared. My home-work was comprehensive and it paid off. I remember in the course of the programme, during an exchange with Kenneth Clarke, then number two at the Depart-ment of Health, I stated how little low-paid health workers received as a basic wage – a figure which he denied. Counterclaims went on for several more minutes, at which point I pulled out of my pocket a hospital porter's payslip, which I asked Robin Day to read out. Kenneth Clarke was for once speechless. There was no answer. The audience enjoyed it and I believe it helped ensure that I was invited back on to the programme on subsequent occasions.

My nervousness had diminished by the time I made my second appearance on *Question Time*, although the unexpected has a disconcerting habit of recurring. I well remember once when Robin Day's introduction at the start of the programme was drowned out by the sound of Teddy noisily lapping water from a bowl and the audience's laughter. A further programme, con-versely, started well, but became tedious as it progressed. By the time we reached the final question, I could sense the audience's boredom with the whole proceedings, so, when Robin turned to me and, in his usual urbane fashion, asked, 'Mr Blunkett, what have you got to say about this question?' I simply responded truthfully, 'Well, my dog's gone to sleep.' The audience understood exactly and brought the house down.

These were not, however, the sole instances when Teddy made an impression. One of my duties as Leader of Sheffield City Council was to meet visiting dignitaries. Among our most memorable guests at the Town Hall were the Queen and Prince Philip, who were to mingle fairly informally with prominent local figures over a cup of tea. As can be imagined, the royal visit was preceded by a period of intense activity as preparations were made, even going so far as confirming with the Palace the precise blend of tea preferred by the royal party. Shortly before the limousine rolled up to the main entrance, I took the precaution of tasting the royal brew. It was awful – far too strong and obviously made in an urn. Hastily I asked for fresh tea to be made. The honour of Sheffield was at stake!

At that moment I was advised that the Queen had arrived. Introductions were made and the royal couple proceeded to mingle with the other guests. We all stood around like wallflowers holding our cups of tea and waiting to be approached by a royal personage. As the Queen moved round the room, I waited pensively. Teddy, with his long legs and magisterial bearing, had no such polite inhibitions. As the Queen approached, in the belief that the cup in the Queen's hand was being offered to him, Teddy thrust his head forward to take a look. There followed a momentary flurry of activity. The Queen hastily withdrew her cup and calamity was avoided by a whisker. The Queen, being an experienced dog owner, was perfectly equal to the situation. Indeed, if Her Majesty recalls anything at all about that visit to Sheffield, it will probably be Teddy and nobody else.

Teddy's behaviour at the royal tea party was a forgivable lapse in his otherwise exemplary behaviour. Unlike Ruby, he caused me remarkably few moments of anxiety in the course of what was, for a guide dog, an exceptionally long and demanding existence.

Having by this time had a guide dog for many years, coping without Teddy when we went on family holidays abroad was not easy. I had always vowed I would not become dependent on a dog and to this end would maintain my skills in using sound, touch and imagination. They had not disappeared, but the easy confidence derived from working with a dog certainly made managing without one a strain. Even after so many years of marriage, Ruth was never entirely at ease with the business of guiding me. There was one particular holiday incident, however, where even Teddy's presence could not have prevented what was very nearly a fatal accident in France in the summer of 1982.

While other friends and their children drove to the holiday complex not far from Bordeaux, we made the journey by train. It was a hot, dusty August afternoon when we arrived, and we were all feeling slightly frayed at the edges. Ruth, who was pregnant, led the way up the stairs to our rented apartment. I followed with two-year-old Hugh on my shoulders, while five-year-old Alastair trailed along behind, grumbling at the exertion. The flat turned out to be dark and Spartan so it was a relief to be able to join our friends camping near by and spend the day on the beach.

It was very hot and the sea, though rough, was

inviting. I went swimming while the others sunbathed. On dry land there are always identifiable features by which I can orientate myself, even though I cannot see them. When swimming in a calm sea, it is still relatively easy to discern the direction of the beach by listening for the waves lapping on the shore, but a cacophony of rough breakers with conflicting currents and strong undertow is an entirely different matter. Within minutes I became totally disorientated and began swimming straight out to sea. Had it not been for the prompt action of Helen Jackson's son, Ben, who bravely swam after me and managed to shout directions, disaster might not have been averted since I was well out of my depth and tiring fast. Fortunately I was none the worse for the experience once I had recovered.

I rarely worry about the potential dangers of not being able to see because it might deter me from doing the normal, everyday things which make life worthwhile. By accepting challenges, I can prove to myself that I am no different and can take on the world just like anyone else. It was a relief, though, to be back in Britain, and reunited with Teddy once more. He had enjoyed a holiday of his own at the Guide Dog Centre in Bolton.

Politicians are often accused of being strong on family values in theory, but weak in practice. My own commitment was tested on 31 October 1982, the day my third son was born. This was also the day when a wide-ranging, international symposium on apartheid and anti-racism, organised under the auspices of the United Nations, was to commence in Sheffield. Among those attending were leading members of the African National Congress, including Oliver Tambo, and representatives of all the leading nations working with and under the direction of the UN. A formal dinner had been arranged in the evening to welcome the guests – a dinner at which, as Leader of the Council, I was to be one of the principal speakers. As it transpired, however, this was one of those instances when politics had to take second place: I spent the evening at Jessop Hospital welcoming my new son into the world. Then a tiny sprig of a baby, he is now a strong lad full of health and vigour. Despite the urgings of many conference delegates next day to name the baby after Nelson Mandela, whom I admired greatly, I stuck to my guns: Andrew Keir it was to be – Keir after Keir Hardie and Andrew for himself.

Some years later, when in Parliament, I was to discover how difficult it was going to be to persuade people that looking after the family and sometimes putting them before politics are very important. There have been times since when my resolve has been tested and I have had to incur some political wrath for putting the boys first, although there is no question that spending so much time in London and on political campaigning does take its toll.

Trips to London became an increasingly regular feature of my life – and Teddy's – following my election in 1983 to the National Executive Committee (NEC) of the Labour Party. I was very pleased to be elected, firstly because I was the first non-Parliamentarian to be elected to the rank-and-file constituency section since Harold Laski, the renowned Professor of Politics at the London School of Economics during the forties and Party Chairman in 1945, and secondly because I enjoyed being involved in national politics. The years between 1983 and my election to Parliament in 1987 proved to be a particularly interesting and formative period as a member of the executive. At this stage the leadership needed every vote it could get to carry key motions, especially when we were dealing with Militant Tendency in 1985–6.

I remember one visit to London in particular when Neil Kinnock invited me to stay the night with him and Glenys at their home in Ealing. I accepted the offer as a gesture of friendship since I had no regular base of my own in London then, but did jokingly point out that the way I chose to vote would depend solely on the arguments put forward the next day and not on the offer of a bed. The following morning, while I was showering before breakfast, and listening to Neil's racking early-morning cough, my ablutions were suddenly interrupted by a yell from Glenys downstairs in the kitchen. Hastily towelling myself dry, I dressed and rushed down to see if I could help, by which time Glenys and Neil were sipping coffee calmly and chatting away. When I asked why she had yelled out, Glenys reassured me that it was not a catastrophe – merely that she had been trying to prevent Teddy from devouring their cat's bowl of food. Shades of Ruby. Quite out of character, Teddy had evidently felt that the cat food was eminently more tasty than his dried Febo.

There are a number of friends who have stuck by me over the years and who, in those days, offered a bed for the night. Elisabeth and Donald Hoodless (Elisabeth is Director of Community Service Volunteers, of which I have been a trustee for over twenty years), Margaret and Henry Hodge (Margaret was Leader of Islington Council), Jean Corston (then a national organiser of the Labour Party and now MP for Bristol East), and Tessa

Jowell and her husband, David. Tessa took over from me as Chairman of the Association of Metropolitan Authorities and is now MP for Dulwich, and helped with the development of Labour's Health policy when she entered Parliament in 1992.

At this time the task of leading the Labour Party was very difficult, owing to the continual splits and divisions. I like to think I played my part in trying to act as a bridge between the non-Militant Left and the leadership. Together with Tom Sawyer, now General Secretary of the Labour Party, but then representing NUPE, and Michael Meacher, a longstanding friend, I did my best to put across the message that we were in one party, even though we had our differences and genuinely held alternative points of view. In some respects, this position of holding the balance, even for a short time, probably gave me an inflated sense of my own importance, but it also engendered in me a real appreciation of the political responsibility we were carrying. The situation certainly gave me an opportunity to exercise influence in a way which would not normally have been the case.

In 1984 I was elected Chairman of the NEC Local Government Committee and by late that year I was at the forefront of the councils who were struggling to combat the Tory Government's capping of rates and major cutbacks in services. As Chairman of the Local Government Campaign Unit, which drew together councils and trade unions, I had to try and hold the ring between those endeavouring to do a deal with the Government and a handful of people playing at revolutionary politics.

Crisis after crisis seemed to threaten during that year and the next. At the Labour Party Conference in Bournemouth in October 1985 the actions of Militant

Tendency members in Liverpool were on everyone's minds. Neil Kinnock attacked them in an excellent speech, conjuring forth the image of Labour councillors scuttling round in taxis delivering redundancy notices. It was a bravura performance. The following day it was my turn to address the conference and, in the course of denouncing Militant Tendency, I challenged Derek Hatton, Deputy Leader of Liverpool, to open the books of Liverpool City Council so that an inquiry into their finances could be organised. I was as surprised as the rest of the audience when, showman that he is, Derek made his way to the rostrum, took the microphone and agreed to my demand.

I believe that, at the time, Neil Kinnock thought I had let him down by bringing about a change of atmosphere in the conference hall. I think he thought I had let Militant off the hook, whereas, as he later generously acknowledged, the outcome helped to pull the Labour Party together. Never before had Militant Tendency been forced to agree to open their books and allow us to see precisely what was going on. In due course, financial experts from local government examined the accounts and revealed that Militant had been pulling the wool over the eyes of the Labour Party as well as the people of Liverpool.

Having exposed the truth about what was going on in Liverpool, an investigation was set up by the NEC to look into the membership of Militant Tendency. As a member of the NEC, I was to spend long days at the subsequent hearings. One interview with Tony Mulhearn, Chairman of Liverpool District Labour Party, lasted sixteen hours. Derek Hatton, to the disappointment of a few, did not deign to attend when summoned before us and so was expelled in his absence.

Frequent attendance at these and other NEC meetings in the Palace of Westminster not only acquainted Teddy and me with the corridors of power but also established us as old hands on the Inter-City trains between Sheffield and London. It was in the course of one such trip that a disagreement took place when a couple of fellow passengers insisted on feeding titbits to Teddy against my wishes. Nowadays people tend to be more sensitive and ask before feeding my dog – a request which must always be refused. Apart from the dog's weight, it creates an expectation that people will offer him food, which is unfair all round, as it turns the dog into a pest. On this particular occasion, the people took exception when I remonstrated with them. Finally, annoyed, I asked how they would like it if I were to put sugar in the petrol tank of their car. They were rather taken aback at this, but did seem at last to grasp the point that they were disrupting Teddy's ability to work properly. I make this point not simply to discourage people from feeding guide dogs but so that they understand the reasons why.

On our many journeys together, Teddy travelled with equanimity in almost every conceivable form of transport. When we flew from London to Glasgow and then on to Inverness on a small island-hopping plane, Teddy took it all in his stride, lying quietly on the floor beneath my seat, apparently unaware of the admiration of fellow passengers and crew.

Since it is not feasible to take a guide dog out of Britain, given the length of time the animal would have to spend in quarantine upon return, working trips abroad have by necessity involved my being accompanied by someone from my office. An experienced assistant who knows my ways and needs is vital if I am to avoid the

tension and awkwardness inevitable in a strange environment, especially in a non-English-speaking country.
She can let me know where objects are located, inform
me precisely who people are, where they are standing
and when hands are being proffered. She can also give
me a verbal picture of our surroundings, keep me in
touch with what is happening and fill me in on anything
of interest. It is important that this assistance is given
in such a way that others are unaware of it so that I can
work effectively. When travelling abroad as part of a
group or delegation, it is not possible to rely on political
colleagues for the type of continuous back-up needed
in such situations; they have their own priorities and
concerns.

Many blind people maintain that independence
when travelling abroad does not matter, that part of the
pleasure is having to make acquaintances by asking
for help. I understand their view, but do not share it.
Being dependent on strangers or on other members of
a contingent does not appeal to me. I prefer to live and
work as independently as possible, otherwise it is easy
for others to underestimate one's abilities and serious
intentions.

In most respects, however, foreign travel poses no
more problems for me than for any other traveller. On
the contrary, I may perhaps enjoy a few advantages. After
years of experience derived from handling negotiations
and participating in meetings without visual signals to
guide me, I have learned to listen particularly carefully,
not only to the spoken word but for other signs. I can
sense the vibrations given off by someone who is tense
or distracted. There are also other clues to pick up: the
rustle of someone shifting in a chair, an intake of breath,
as well as the length of a pause and the quality of a

silence. Of course I may sometimes misconstrue these signals, but then so do sighted people.

The issue of understanding the culture and manners of different nations seems to me an interesting one because the British in general appear to be very poor in this regard. In 1983, when Sheffield twinned with the city of Anshan, a major steel and iron producing centre in north-east China, I led a delegation of officials and businessmen on a visit to the city. The group as a whole found it difficult to understand and adhere to Chinese customs, whether it was manners, method of negotiation or forms of address. For instance, when speaking to our Chinese counterparts, in order to avoid causing offence, we had to learn to express ourselves in a more effusive manner than we would at home. Thus a conversation might open along the lines of, 'We are very honoured to be here with you and have the opportunity to learn about your wonderful country, this fine city and the enormous strides you've made in recent years . . .' This does not require sight to appreciate, merely an understanding of the fact that, as a guest in someone else's country, it is necessary to respond courteously and respect their customs.

Rather more successful, in several respects, was a trip to the United States when, within the space of a week, I visited Los Angeles, Washington and New York. In Los Angeles we looked at volunteer programmes which had been developed in Watts Labour Community, a black neighbourhood. This was followed by a flight to Washington, where we paid a rapid visit to the State Department before flying on to New York for discussions with their equivalent of our Community Service Volunteers. On the day we were due to leave, light snow was falling as we made our way to the Town Hall for our final meeting. When we left by taxi for FAO Schwartz, the famous toy store, to buy presents for the boys, the snow was falling thick and fast. By the time we emerged from the shop, there was a foot of snow and the city was at a virtual standstill. We returned to the hotel to hear that Kennedy Airport was closed, thus affording an extra day in which to explore New York. It was this which was to provide me with two outstanding memories of that brief visit.

The first occurred while we were standing on the quay waiting for the boat to take us over to Liberty Island and the Statue. Standing in the open air on that freezing January day, I very clearly 'felt' the New York skyline. It is hard to describe, but from the sound of the ships' horns reverberating off the skyscrapers on the water-front, I could picture the skyline: the sheer height of the World Trade Center, the chasms of streets between the towering buildings, the sheer vastness of it all.

My second vivid memory is of Central Park on the morning following the previous day's heavy snow, buzzing with life and energy, a vast playground-cum-sports field where New Yorkers turned out in their thousands to jog, skate and ski. Yet there are also woodland walks, wildlife and quiet ways where total tranquillity can be found. We drank hot chocolate by the skating rink and watched a very old man skating alongside all the youngsters. It struck me that, for a short while at least, on the ice he was as young as they were, could match their speed and feel youthful again. The whole scene made a deep impression on me and I put my thoughts on paper: a blind man visualising and attempting to encapsulate in poetry a scene he could 'see' and feel as deeply as someone who could see it for himself.

An old man skates across the ice
Bent of back
But moving as in youth.
The music plays and winter is alive.

A squirrel scurries on the snow,
The crisp white carpet
Showing no footprints
No sign of the City.

This is Central Park, New York.
A place of white and glitter,
When winter blizzards piled up snow
And held us in its timelessness.

Skyscrapers on the skyline
Sun catching our faces
Capturing the spirit
Of a city wanting us to stay.

We contemplate the contradictions
Of this vibrant city
Of life and movement
Of wealth and desperate poverty

Whose turmoil seems to beat
Vibrant and strong
Like a youthful heart
Fed by the adrenaline of life.

Unexpected events were not solely limited to business trips: family holidays were also capable of engendering them. With the arrival of Andrew in the family, there were now five disparate temperaments to try to please when it came to planning holidays. At my insistence, and with rare exceptions, we went away for a week at

Easter as well as two weeks each summer with friends and their children. When not venturing abroad, we might rent a cottage in Norfolk or one year we stayed on the coast near St David's in South Wales.

I was very keen to try my hand at sea fishing which holds no difficulties for a blind person other than baiting the line. It is possible to feel the fish bite and to reel in, playing the fish by touch and listening for it flapping in time to hoist it over the edge of the boat. Perhaps a little assistance with disgorging might be necessary. I remember one occasion when, after several days of bad weather, we eventually succeeded in getting a trip out on the last day of our holiday. Twenty mackerel in the bag and the prospect of a tasty supper – or so I thought – only to return to the cottage to find that the rest of them had already bought fish and chips.

A very different holiday was spent in 1985 when we headed off to Brittany. After the stress of battling against Militant and with central government on restrictions on local government spending and rate capping, by the time August came I could not wait to escape, especially as it had proved impossible for me to accompany the rest of the family to Spain the previous Easter. A rented house on an exposed and empty stretch of the north coast of Brittany promised to be an ideal spot in which to wind down. The first untoward incident occurred when I decided to take advantage of the fact that there was nobody else around on the long, flat beach and try my hand at driving our car. Had the police officer who many years before accused me of driving a Mini been there at that moment, he would have had his worst fears realised. No guide dog in the back – only three excited small boys and an increasingly exasperated wife whose irritation turned to anger when I stalled the car within a few feet of the water's edge, with the carburettor flooded and the tide rising fast. It was an awkward situation. The car had glided smoothly enough over the sand when the engine was running, but pushing its dead weight back up the wet beach was no easy task. In the event, we managed to restart the engine only as the sea lapped the front tyres.

Whatever else is said about family holidays, no one can say they are without incident. Later in the same holiday we had a second close call. It was a sunny day on the beach and the breeze had made the sea choppy, but not too rough for swimming. The boys and I were playing in the water. Alastair, by then eight years old, had learned to swim, while Hugh, aged five, and Andrew, aged three, were bobbing around in a small plastic inflatable boat, which I controlled by a length of thin rope. As I waded out through the waves, Andrew and Hugh paddled away frantically, heading for the open sea. Out and out we went until I was swimming. They were laughing as they bounced on the swell. Then, suddenly, Hugh cried out: 'Dad, we're going down.'

'What do you mean you're going down?' I gasped, trying to tread water.

'We're sinking, Dad,' came the plaintive response.

Frantically I swam towards the boat while at the same time hauling them in on the rope and discovered that they were indeed sinking. The air was escaping rapidly from what was anyway a flimsy craft. Clutching the deflating plastic in one hand, I began swimming towards the shallows. Alastair, meanwhile, was shouting to me so that I did not head off in the wrong direction. The plastic dinghy was by now waterlogged. With Hugh and Andrew clinging to me, it seemed an eternity before I felt the reassuring firmness of sand beneath my feet and I was able to deposit them safely back on the beach.

Although it is hard to put my finger on it now, somehow during this same holiday I realised that Ruth and I were not going to last as a married couple. The belief that it was better for us to stay together in order to care for the boys had kept the marriage afloat long after I had ceased to hope that my youthful dreams might be fulfilled. I recall one afternoon in St Malo, sitting in a busy square feeling very lonely. Yet these days, although I live alone, I never feel lonely. In fact St Malo is exactly the sort of place where I would now be quite content to sit and absorb the atmosphere of the lovely old town.

9

Pawprints in the House

'CAN HE POSSIBLY become an MP?' was a question not infrequently voiced in the Labour Party when the possibility of my standing for selection as the candidate for Sheffield Brightside was first mooted in 1985. In spite of having been Leader of Sheffield City Council for five years and being on the national political scene for some time, there were people who still had lingering doubts that anyone with a 'disability' could do the job. Yet, once again, the local party took a risk and adopted me as its official candidate, for which I was extremely grateful.

The weeks leading up to the 1987 General Election were spent exhaustively pounding the constituency, drumming up support. In addition, I had been co-opted as a member of the Party's General Election campaign team. This was not as influential a position as might at first appear, since there was in reality an inner circle who made key decisions, and those of us who were called together every two or three days were there merely to ratify what had already been settled. My efforts to get the threat of water privatisation and the impending poll tax, already in place in Scotland, higher on our scale of priorities came to nothing.

The truth of the matter is that while the campaign

appealed to the media, it did not appeal to the ordinary potential Labour voters. The notion that the 'medium is the message' is nonsense. Certainly the public's perception of a political party and the nature of a political debate can be influenced through sustained, broadly based efforts by both print and broadcast journalism, but Margaret Thatcher was living proof that conviction and clear appeal to an identified segment of the population can be extremely effective. The siren voices of those whose interests lie in defending power and privilege will always move the goal posts no matter how far Labour changes. This is why I have stuck to the belief that being a modern and forward-looking party makes downright common sense, and yet the maintenance of core values and beliefs is just as crucial if people are to trust Labour, know what we stand for and believe that we mean business when in government. The people's interests have to be our interests and vice versa. But the small matter of how to bring about change and how to challenge those who always resist change, unless it is in their own interests, were questions we in the Labour Party failed to address. It was to be another eight years before we won over a substantial swathe of the electorate. So it was that in 1987 one could palpably feel that Labour were not making progress in winning new voters, no matter how hard we tried or how slick the party political broadcasts.

Late on 11 June, when all the votes had been counted and the Returning Officer announced that I had been duly elected to serve as Member of Parliament for Sheffield Brightside, I felt a mixture of conflicting emotions. Pride and elation, naturally, but my feelings of anticipation were tinged with a certain regret. Life would in many ways never be the same again. The immediate aftermath of the election passed in a haze of interviews, meetings and plans. Shortly after the State Opening of Parliament on 25 June 1987, I made my maiden speech – the first new member to do so in the new Parliament.

Some months earlier Ruth and I had reluctantly come to the mutual decision to separate. She and the boys were to remain in the family home, while in due course I would seek another house in Sheffield large enough for the lads to stay at weekends. I was taken aback to find that I was pursued by a reporter from the *Sunday Mirror*, the northern edition of which featured the story of our separation on the front page – this despite the fact that no third party was involved and there was no word of recrimination from either Ruth or myself. This brought home to me how difficult it would be in the future to maintain any privacy.

It was a fraught and unhappy period for all the family, and it is at such times that good friends come into their own, not least my four-legged companion who took on London with me. Teddy was a workaholic, which made us well matched. Both of us needed all the reserves of energy and determination we could muster to meet the various changes and challenges that I knew we would have to face over the coming year.

By this stage, Teddy had been with me for the best part of nine years and was already well known in the Palace of Westminster. Having learned by trial and error to find our way through the vast maze of corridors and staircases, we had soon mastered our regular routes sufficiently to allow us to go about our business with reasonable confidence and aplomb. With my election as an MP, Teddy was set to become the first dog allowed on the floor of the Commons' chamber proper.

There was, however, a dark cloud hanging over us: Teddy's declining health due to old age. Could he withstand the long hours and pressure of my first year in Parliament? Even at the age of eleven, his commitment and loyalty made him as eager as ever for work. Whenever the lead and harness were taken off their hook, he would be beside me, putting his head into his harness rather than waiting for me to pass it over his head. It was deeply touching. He was determined not to be left at home or to give up. He was less robust than in his youth and slightly stiffer in the joints, but otherwise not in bad shape.

After soul-searching discussions with the GDBA, and since the vet assured me that Teddy was in no serious discomfort, it was agreed that he should continue working as long as he was keen to do so. Teddy knew his way around and the close bond we had formed over the years would make the unenviable stresses of the year ahead less arduous.

In January 1988, I began serving on a Commons' Standing Committee, consisting of a majority of Tories, with Labour and Liberal in proportion to the Members in the House. The task was to scrutinise the first draft of the Local Government Finance Bill, in which domestic rates were to be replaced by Mrs Thatcher's community charge or poll tax. This was a long and complex Bill, which led to some of the most hard-fought committee sessions in the history of the House. We sat late into the night, often until three or four o'clock in the morning, arguing through the Bill clause by clause. All these long sessions, which Teddy shared, came on top of our regular working day. As the weeks turned into months, tiredness took its toll: I was struck down with viral pneumonia, which led to a spell in hospital. This was my second period in hospital since entering the House, as the previous November I had had my gall bladder removed. Without the care and comfort of my close friends at this time, it would have been difficult to withstand the stress of this period, let alone come through it more determined than ever to succeed.

Equally, had it not been for the fact that I was forced to spend time in hospital recuperating, thereby providing an enforced rest for Teddy, I doubt whether he could have gone on working for me as long as he did, for by this time I had noticed he was beginning to slow down. I left hospital in March 1988 under doctor's orders to take things easy, and in the weeks that followed Teddy and I made our way round Westminster looking for all the world like a pair of geriatrics.

Then one hot, humid day in the middle of May, I noticed that Teddy was panting, not abnormally at first, but as the day faded and the air temperature dropped, he seemed to grow much worse. Desperately concerned, I carried him out of the Palace of Westminster and took him in a taxi to the nearest vet.

The prognosis could scarcely have been worse. Teddy's heart and circulation were failing – he had only a few weeks to live. I literally dropped everything and with a heavy heart took Teddy by train back to Sheffield. There I left him with Valda and Trevor, who I knew would love and care for him. Having settled Teddy with them, I reluctantly returned to London, where I tried my best to concentrate on the tasks in hand. It was not easy.

On 5 July, as the House of Commons was debating a motion on the fortieth anniversary of the National Health Service, I was given a message that Teddy had been rushed to the vet after collapsing and losing the use of his legs. The vet felt that he had at last come to the end of the road and that it would be kinder to put him to sleep. I had to return home at once. Without waiting for permission to be absent from the vote, I caught the next train north. When I arrived at the surgery, Teddy tried to get to his feet and I will never forget the sound of his paws scrabbling on the bare lino of the surgery floor. My heart went out to him. Despite some reluctance on the part of the vet, I managed to persuade him to allow us to take Teddy home to familiar surroundings. I did not want Teddy's days to end there in that surgery.

Once out of the car Teddy found the strength from somewhere to make his own way into the house and on to his favourite rug. When the vet arrived a couple of hours later, I cradled Teddy's head in my lap and gently fondled his ears as he was put to sleep. There is a lump in my throat as I write even after all this time. I have to admit that on that evening, with all the memories of Teddy flooding back, I became the sentimentalist I had so scorned in others twenty years earlier, before I had a dog.

> He was a gentle giant of a dog,
> Running magnificent through the woods,
> A huge branch clamped between his teeth.
>
> He was a soft, lovable lion of a dog,
> Full of sniffs and a nuzzling nose,
> Touching against the hand
> To say thank you for walks
> And for fondling of ears.
>
> He was a *Guinness Book of Records* dog,
> First ever in the Chamber,

Enduring the noise and bad behaviour
Of the 'schoolboys',
And the medieval ritual of the Mother of
    Parliaments.

He was a TV star dog,
Sleeping through *Question Time*,
Lifting his head only when it was time to go,
And bringing a smile to millions
And joy to those who knew him well.

A child could climb upon his back
Or pull his ears without fear or threat,
For Teddy was a dog of love, you see,
Who cared for others as he cared for me.

Guiding me, wherever I needed to be,
Full of keenness, enthusiasm and love of life,
Working to a record age
And giving of his best, wherever we might be.

Being superb – my guide dog gave his all
In those twelve years, you see.
And all of us who knew him
Will remember him with gratitude,
And with love and much affection.

In the days following Teddy's death, as the news
spread, many kind friends and colleagues expressed
their condolences, but none was more unexpected than
a handwritten message from Margaret Thatcher saying
how sorry she was that Teddy had died and that she
understood what a great loss it would be for me, not
only for practical reasons but also for the loss of the
enormous affection guide dogs have for their owners.
To my regret, I never had the opportunity to debate

politics with Margaret Thatcher, but she did have a passing acquaintance with Teddy and would always pat him on the head when she passed, so perhaps her letter should not have come as such as surprise. Iron Lady she might have been, but she did have a soft spot for Teddy.

Teddy had become equally widely known outside Parliament and so many sacks of letters arrived from sympathetic members of the public that a fund was set up in his memory. This raised over £7,600 for the GDBA and helped provide training for several new guide dogs, one of whom was to be named Teddy. I am sure 'the gentle giant' would have liked that since he had no sons of his own.

The GDBA normally tells a prospective owner very little about the guide dog to be assigned to him or her before arriving at the training centre. I was therefore grateful when the Association decided that, given the unusual demands of my job and the high profile any dog of mine would inevitably have, it was sensible to talk through the kind of dog I needed.

Teddy's loyal service during my first year as MP had allowed the GDBA time to seek out and train an appropriate successor. I was informed that my new dog was to be a German Shepherd/golden retriever cross by the name of Uffa. Guide dogs are named in alphabetical order per litter, thus Uffa and all his siblings had names beginning with U. To be honest, I did not care for the name. The only Uffa I had heard of was Uffa Fox, the famous sailor, and I could predict puzzled expressions and long explanations ahead. I therefore asked whether it might be possible to rename him Offa, which would be easier to explain. Offa, King of Mercia, just over one thousand years ago, was responsible for ordering the construction of Offa's Dyke, the fortification along the border between England and Wales, and for developing the pound sterling as common currency for the area over which he had jurisdiction. A completely different sounding name would have been totally out of the question because it would have interrupted his training, but the GDBA were quite happy for this slight change to be made. So Offa it was.

Another helpful concession made by the GDBA was that, since this was to be my third guide dog and the pressure of work was acute, I only had to spend eight days at the training centre. This was not a unique concession, though rare at that time. There were, in fact, two other owners on this short course who were returning for replacement dogs and had particular problems: Gail O'Hara, who had recently undergone a kidney transplant after many years of illness, and Sue Mann, a mother of two small children, who needed her at home.

Taking on a new dog is not as easy as it might appear. Although basically the same, each trainer has different techniques and perhaps uses slightly different commands, while of course each dog has its own individual temperament. On top of which, I myself had inevitably acquired some bad habits over the years with Ruby and Teddy, and these needed to be eliminated or modified when dealing with a new dog – rather like someone who has been driving for ten years having to retake a driving test. It was a highly intensive training period, with the need to absorb information very quickly.

So it was that in August 1988 I was requested to attend Middlesbrough training centre on Teesside to meet my new partner, Offa. I could not have wished for a more lively dog, full of bounce. All the kennel staff and others at the centre thought Offa was wonderful, certainly one of their favourites. Becoming accustomed to him as a guide dog was, however, a different matter. Like Teddy in his youth, Offa seemed to have inbuilt booster rockets which meant he would shoot off at a rate of knots with me clinging for dear life to the harness, trying to slow him down. I was out of practice and had to rediscover muscles long out of use.

While we were training, I first discovered Offa's fascination for younger or smaller animals of most varieties, especially furry ones. Jim Powell, Offa's trainer, recently reminded me of the day a television crew arrived to interview me about my new dog. In the course of the recording, Offa became transfixed by the fur cover on the large microphone, which, being a novice in such matters at that time, he evidently mistook for an animal. As soon as the microphone was pushed under my nose, Offa started to creep towards it and then began to bark, to the great consternation of the camera crew and sound recordist. A brief training session followed to ensure that it did not happen again.

One unexpected bonus of having been ill and therefore absent so much during my first year in Parliament was that my fellow MPs were spared my 'over-enthusiasm', which might have led to irritation on their part. I had arrived believing that I could step from being a big fish in the relatively small pond of the political arena in Sheffield into this new one, expecting to be instantly accepted. As I learned to my cost, this turned out not to be the case. Like Ken Livingstone and my longstanding friend Margaret Hodge, among others, I experienced distrust and resentment from a number of fellow MPs, not only because of my perceived reputation but also because I had not yet had to endure, as they had, the grind of spending years in Opposition inside the House of Commons.

With Offa, in a sense, I began life afresh in the Palace of Westminster. Such a magisterial figure as he had little difficulty settling into Westminster and making friends. These included Michael Meacher, always a favourite because Offa associated him with being given a lift home, Joan Walley, who for many years had the office next to mine, Clare Short, who would always make a fuss of him, and from the Tory benches, Dame Janet Fookes. One way or another, Offa had an enviably diverse range of friends and admirers.

Offa's most appealing aspects were undoubtedly his willingness to do the job and his keen desire to please, both of which had a tendency to lead to over-zealous response. For instance, if I said, 'Find the door', he would find it at fifty miles an hour. He was highly possessive and liked to be the centre of attention, a trait typical of the German Shepherd in him. If someone else appeared to be attracting too much notice from me, he would grow jealous and try to impose himself upon me. The interesting thing was that he could obviously distinguish between work and leisure because this behaviour was never apparent in the House. I was very fond of Offa, but recognised very early in our partnership that spoiling him or indulging him too much would lead to difficulties; I had to be kind and fair – but firm.

While Ruby and Teddy had both adored swimming, Offa did not. Given his strong build, I think he would have made a good swimmer, but luckily for me he had no interest in water whatsoever. In fact, once when I was on holiday, Offa was taken by the GDBA, together with a number of younger trainee guide dogs, on an outing to a lake. While the other dogs romped and retrieved sticks from the water, Offa sat imperiously on the bank, guarding the pile of discarded harnesses and gear, and watching indulgently as the soaking trainees enjoyed themselves. 'He looked for all the world like King Offa surveying his subjects,' said one of the guide-dog trainers.

One of Offa's first public duties was to accompany me to the annual Labour Party Conference in October 1988. This turned out to be a particularly gruelling experience because I had been asked to speak from the platform on behalf of the National Executive Committee in a debate on the poll tax. The main issue was whether or not the Party should recommend to all its members and supporters that they pay the tax – even though we vehemently opposed it – but the NEC believed that our campaign against the poll tax would be instrumental in the wider campaign to remove the Government from office. If people refused to pay, it would merely accelerate a deterioration of essential services and thus undermine public confidence in those services. Those who do not believe in public provision and are instead committed to forcing people to 'go private' were hardly likely to shed any tears over local authorities failing to collect the money, vital to pay wages and maintain services.

At the end of the debate, the conference vote swung in the NEC's favour and over the following two years, until Margaret Thatcher's downfall, I had the job of helping organise one of the most successful campaigns in British political history. In the end, however, Michael Heseltine effectively defeated both Mrs Thatcher and the poll tax, which cost Labour the next

General Election and ensured the Tories a narrow but adequate victory in 1992.

Labour's National Executive Committee gathered in May 1989 for a memorable two-day session at Transport House, the head office of the TGWU in Smith Square, formerly the Labour Party headquarters. Mike Lee, my then policy research and press officer, accompanied me. The meeting was important because the NEC was to approve a document entitled 'Meet the Challenge, Make the Change', a major review of Labour's policy which was to be the turning point in Neil Kinnock's efforts to modernise the Party. Although later documents were produced which watered down and slightly altered what had been agreed, for the following three years this formed the foundation of Labour's policy. 'Meet the Challenge' offered a truly radical alternative and many excellent ideas which, if updated and progressed, would have helped us towards that elusive General Election victory. However, the very fact that almost three years elapsed before the next General Election was also to prove the document's biggest disadvantage.

During tea breaks, Mike and I would take Offa out for much-needed fresh air and physical relief. The sole green spot appropriate for this purpose was the grass outside St John's Church, where an irate clergyman promptly spotted us and rushed over to insist that, guide dog or not, there was to be no fouling of his patch of green and pleasant land. From this I deduced that whatever else his virtues, he was not a descendant of St Francis of Assisi. (Some years later, Mike married Helen Shreeve whom he met while she was working for me and I like to think I played a part in bringing them together.)

One of the major issues debated during the two-day session was Labour's defence policy. In the course of debate, there was considerable cut and thrust in which I found myself on the opposite side to many good colleagues, such as Robin Cook, Clare Short and, of course, Neil Kinnock. Central and Eastern Europe were about to throw off the yoke of totalitarianism and change was enveloping the world. At that precise moment, Labour reversed its non-nuclear stance.

Looking back, I believe the defence debate was probably not as relevant as once it might have been because the focus of the attention had shifted elsewhere. As a consequence, Neil's gesture to the British electorate was viewed by press and public more in terms of an abandonment of principle and another untrustworthy change of policy rather than a move towards Labour's electability.

Poor old Offa had to sit out these two days with infrequent breaks and I am sure he sensed my frustration when, on the second morning, I found that overnight some guileless member of the TGWU had disposed of my braille copy of the meeting document and all my braille notes, as well as a good set of earphones.

In January 1990, I accepted an Industry and Parliament Trust placement. This involved spending time over the next eighteen months with a major company – in this instance, British Telecom – investigating the workings of senior management and compiling a report of my findings, positive and negative. During my time as Leader of Sheffield City Council, I had actively learned a substantial amount about telecommunications, so the placement proved interesting. As a result, I came to the conclusion that if government ministers had had the same opportunity they might not have blundered into allowing the American-owned cable companies to dig up our roads and pavements in the most expensive duplication of communications facilities imaginable. Ten years after we made our recommendations from Sheffield, Britain embarked on the wrong cabling for the wrong reasons.

Later the same year, Ruth and I were finally divorced. Alastair, Hugh and Andrew coped with this painful experience very bravely. When people talk today of 'one-parent families', they often misuse the phrase. Many – regrettably not enough – are in fact two-parent families, but the parents are living apart. As in our case, each home offers a loving and welcoming environment for the children. I personally count myself very fortunate to be able to provide a comfortable home for the boys to spend time with me at weekends and during the parliamentary recesses, and we all get along extremely well together.

Alastair is now a young man and he often prepares huge cooked breakfasts for us on Sunday mornings. Hugh likes to bake and tries his hand at anything. He has made bread, croissants, banana cakes and chocolate eclairs, but his forte is his chocolate cake which is excellent. Andrew, for his part, is quite content to let his brothers do the cooking but does his share of table laying and washing up.

For years we have all been keen Sheffield Wednesday supporters – through the good times and the bad! We travelled to London to see Wednesday beat Manchester United 1–0 and carry home the Rumbelow's Cup in 1991. Of course, there was much rejoicing in Sheffield afterwards. Since this heady success, though, Sheffield Wednesday have not fared so well. Battling in the 1993 FA Cup Final, we finally lost to our fierce rivals Arsenal.

The whole of Sheffield, it seemed, had travelled south to Wembley for the semi-final between Sheffield Wednesday and Sheffield United. It was one of those occasions when Sheffielders were at their best, friendly, at first hopeful and then commiserating. For us, of course, it was celebration all the way back, having beaten United 2-1. We were greeted with a wagging tail and a puzzled look from Offa, who had spent a lovely non-working day with friends, wondering where on earth we had got to.

Finding a balance between home life and work is a constant challenge. Unless detained by an important debate and vote in the Commons, I try to return to Sheffield on a Thursday, even though sometimes it may be very late. My sons always come to stay, usually from Saturday afternoon through to Sunday afternoon, and I look forward very much to having them. They are no paragons of virtue, and obviously we have our ups and downs, but when I hear and read about other families and the problems caused by difficult teenagers, I realise how fortunate I am with my three sons. Over the years, individually or as a trio, they have come with me when I have had to travel to some speaking engagement or other, but the novelty of that experience has begun to pall. Now they are older, they prefer to stay behind and do their own thing. Fortunately, they are perfectly capable of taking care of themselves until I return.

It is difficult to describe the nature of the workload for someone taking on a busy frontbench job. In many ways the task is more daunting being in Opposition than in office because the massive back-up of a government department is not there. For instance, when the poll tax was at its most unpopular, the Department for the Environment set up a computerised secretariat system, where different paragraphs from appropriate letters could be put together at the touch of a key and mailed off to the angry protester. In Opposition, one relies heavily on dedicated staff working at Westminster and in the constituency office.

A lot of time is spent travelling the country, trying to fulfil the invitations to speak at various conferences and meet with representatives of authorities and organisations. Some organisers do not always appreciate that somewhere in the day I have to find time to eat! I remember once travelling for almost three hours to get to a meeting on a very cold, snowy winter's evening. Despite the blizzard, we eventually arrived only to find that the meeting had been abandoned and the 'promised' food had been eaten by those who had presumed the guest was not going to turn up. 'There's a fish and chip shop round the corner,' was the riposte to an enquiry about where we might find something to eat. I was too tired to be angry, but reflected ruefully that those who preach socialism should first practise it.

It is the weekends that pose the biggest problems. It is not merely that there are campaign events virtually every weekend of the year. It is not that one can spend half a day travelling before speaking and answering questions for less than an hour. It is not even that people take us for granted. It is the fact that all this has to be done alongside the enormous avalanche of correspondence which rolls in, not only from the constituency but from every part of the country.

Some politicians choose to send standard replies. I have always felt obliged to answer people who have taken the time and trouble to write to me and to do so in a way which respects their views. This does, of course, take its toll. I receive mail in both my London and Sheffield offices. Each piece of correspondence has to be read onto tape, to which I dictate my reply, ensuring sensitivity to the issues raised. When I was working in Health, I received correspondence from individuals who felt that their problem was of primary concern. In Education I am dealing inevitably with those who have motivation and commitment and are often to be satisfied only with detailed answers to complicated questions – but intellectual challenge begins to pall at one o'clock in the morning. I have found that some people write to their MPs simply to let off steam and, once they have aired their views, do not always like to be irritated all over again when they receive a robust reply. There may therefore be a case to be made for the standardised thank-you letter. My current thinking is that some of my time would be better spent on other political activities as well as socialising with other MPs, letting them know what I am doing and catching up with their news.

I find it easier to deal with the backlog in the summer when often it is possible to sit outside in the sunshine on a Sunday afternoon. Writing speeches and preparing for the week ahead does not seem such a bind, and my sons find it less intrusive: work and a little relaxation start to blend more easily. The winter is just a long grind as weekdays and weekends merge into one. That is why I become very angry when people talk about MPs taking long holidays.

I am often asked how, with such a packed timetable, my guide dog obtains sufficient exercise. After all, the reasoning goes, the dog and I spend a considerable part of every day, me sitting, my companion lying down, both in meetings or in the Chamber itself. But this is to misunderstand the situation.

In fact, consecutive appointments are frequently held at opposite ends of the Palace of Westminster so we are continually walking hundreds of yards between venues. One way or another we probably cover a fair number of miles each day, and a guide dog with me has a much more eventful and varied life than the average pet at home. Certainly I have never had an overweight dog and I know we are both quite shattered by the time Parliament goes into recess.

There is much nonsense talked about the recess. Once, during a recess, a television journalist even asked me how I spent my time as I passed him on my way to do the third interview that week for national news. The truth is that, for busy frontbench MPs and for those dedicated to serving their constituencies, the recess can be not only just as hectic but also far more productive than sitting on the front benches simply forming an audience or engaging in the equivalent of public school debate. It does irk, therefore, when the media refer to MPs being 'on holiday' simply because Parliament is not sitting. Doing the job properly involves a seven-day week, whether Parliament is sitting or not.

At the beginning of April 1991, I was offered the opportunity to escape briefly from the day-to-day drudgery of the political grindstone. At the same time, I was to learn something of the art of being a broad-caster, how to ask the questions and paint a word picture, instead of my usual role as politician and parrier of questions. The producer of the BBC Radio 4's *Down Your Way* programme asked if I would not only visit Slad, the Cotswold village, which has its own crevice in history etched out by *Cider with Rosie*, but also interview its author, Laurie Lee. My task was to

help Laurie convey to listeners as much as possible of
his life and work, and the surroundings in which we
met: the village caught on the edge of time between
the old and the new, the harshness and the joy of the
Lee family struggling with poverty during the First
World War.

Basking in the warmth of a spring morning, while
seated beside a window in Laurie's lovely home behind
the Woolpack – the pub which hosted the creation
of a dastardly secret of murder and intrigue in the novel
– I could picture that moment at the beginning of the
twentieth century which Laurie Lee describes so poeti-
cally in *Cider with Rosie*, a book which in my opinion
should be compulsory reading. I could picture the
clouds moving from Wales across Gloucestershire to
drop rain on the same trees, valleys and houses that
Laurie remembers from his childhood.

People are always asking me whether it is possible
to visualise things even though I cannot see. Of course
it is. All of us picture things in our mind when we read
books and listen to plays. Anyone reading *Cider with
Rosie* can enter the world caught in a time warp, a
world which no longer exists but which can be sensed
and appreciated by all of us, these generations on. To
walk in the 'Little Valley' and to appreciate that pre-
history still reaches out to us is to understand what
Laurie was writing about.

He touches me, not merely through his descriptions
of landscape, which evoke the majesty and cruelty of
nature, but also through his depiction of the surrounding warmth of humankind – the care and love of his
sisters, the appreciation of womanhood and the love of
family. Outdated though his education may have been,
what he describes as those 'golden nails' of learning

were hammered in sufficiently well to enable him to write in that exquisite style and thereby make a small part of history come alive for millions of readers. It was, therefore, without the slightest hesitation that I ordered cider when I sat down with Laurie at lunchtime in the Woolpack. For a moment, imagination and reality seemed to touch.

I enjoyed my first efforts at broadcasting and felt easier with my politics knowing that at least I might have a potential second string to my bow!

Later that same year, I was brought face to face with the harsh realities of life and the way in which the world has changed over the century. Returning to my Sheffield home from London one night towards the end of October 1991, I let Offa into the garden for a run. Shortly afterwards, I heard fireworks being set off quite close by. Unfortunately, Offa, though fearless in most respects, was terrified by loud bangs. He immediately took off over the fence and disappeared. I am blessed with extremely good neighbours, so Sue and Richard Blackburn, together with Valda and Trevor, helped me search for Offa in the total darkness of the adjoining woodland and neighbouring gardens. He was nowhere to be found.

Some hours later, I received a telephone call from the guide dog centre in Middlesbrough, who told me that someone had contacted them to say that Offa had been hit by a van on the nearby main road. He was seriously injured. The caller and his friends had apparently witnessed the accident and laid Offa in the gutter before astonishingly continuing on their way to the local pub, from where they had telephoned the number shown on Offa's identification disc. In turn I was contacted and so were the police.

In great anxiety we rushed to the main road only to discover Offa had disappeared. There followed several more hours of fruitless searching. By the early hours of the morning, having found no sign of him, we reluctantly agreed to call off the search for the night and begin again at dawn. By 6.30AM I was on the telephone to the local radio stations who agreed to broadcast an SOS, asking for people to be on the look-out for Offa on their way to work.

Some fourteen hours after Offa first went missing, the police rang. I expected the worst, but was told that he was still alive. He had been discovered lying in the front garden of a house three hundred yards from the main road, where he had crawled and remained throughout the cold wet night.

I was overjoyed when at last we were reunited, but horrified to find that he could not even get to his feet. The vet, after checking him over, pronounced that miraculously no bones were broken but that Offa was badly bruised and traumatised. Unbeknown to us at that time, later events were to indicate that he may have suffered some internal damage. For twenty-four hours he lay under the table, occasionally lapping some warm milk. I was loath to leave him, but had little choice. I had to take part in Radio 4's *Any Questions* that day without Offa, but was able to reassure listeners that, despite his absence, he was on the mend. It was six weeks, however, before he was able to walk at his normal speed again and another three before he could resume work.

Once Offa had regained his health, life gradually slipped back into normal gear and our schedule ran as smoothly as it ever does in politics. One weekend, a couple of months before the General Election due to

be held on 9 April 1992, Offa began to vomit continuously. The vet was summoned and at once took Offa
back to his surgery on the outskirts of Sheffield.
Careful examination revealed nothing to indicate a
serious problem and, after a series of injections, Offa
appeared to have recovered.

On 30 March, having spent all day campaigning in
Wales, I booked into a hotel in Bristol for a welcome
night's sleep before resuming the campaign trail in the
Bristol North-West constituency, a seat which, in the
event, we lost by a mere forty-five votes. I went to bed
early but was awakened within an hour by the sound of
Offa panting. He was obviously in severe distress. Had I
been sleeping more soundly, I am convinced that Offa
would have been dead by morning.

With the help of the hotel night staff, I managed to
locate a vet who was willing to see us immediately. It
was a race against time. Although the taxi took only
fifteen minutes to reach the surgery, by the time we
arrived, Offa was in a desperate state, on the verge of
total collapse and barely able to breathe. Paddy March,
the vet, diagnosed gastric torsion, a condition in which
the stomach enlarges and rotates, causing damage to the
internal organs. As Offa was too weak to withstand an
operation immediately, he was sedated and a stomach
tube was inserted to allow decompression, and thus
relieve the immediate danger. An intravenous drip
administered fluids and drugs into his bloodstream.
At this point I was advised to return to the hotel and
contact the surgery in the morning.

Early the following day a complex operation was
carried out, during which Offa's stomach was untwisted
through 270 degrees and damaged portions of the
stomach wall were removed. Three times during the

operation Paddy March and the nurse feared it was hopeless. It was a dreadfully worrying period – I really did not know whether Offa was going to live or die. At lunchtime when I visited, he lay barely conscious, connected to tubes and drips. Gloomily, I stroked his head. He feebly wagged his tail in response. It was a hopeful sign, but only a momentary one. For the following three days, Offa's life hung in the balance, while he suffered heart palpitations caused by the release of poisons into his system from damaged organs. Day and night his condition was monitored. Not until four more days had passed did Offa at last show some signs of improvement.

Ten days later, once Offa had convalesced and undergone dietary management, I returned to Bristol to collect him from the surgery. It was the Saturday following Labour's defeat in the General Election, so at least he had missed the final hectic fortnight of the campaign. It was a minor consolation. Fortunately, the only lasting effect of this ghastly ordeal was that, because a substantial proportion of his stomach had been removed, Offa suffered from a delicate digestion and had to be fed small quantities three times a day on a permanent basis.

Following Labour's General Election defeat, Neil Kinnock resigned and a leadership contest ensued, during which I acted as campaign manager for Bryan Gould. I had come to have a great deal of respect for him over the years and was disappointed when he lost. I did, however, come to have an enormous respect for John Smith as Leader and to appreciate why he was elected so overwhelmingly. It was a sad day when Bryan decided to return to his native New Zealand and I believe his departure was a real loss to the Party and to British politics. I still feel to this day that he ought to have reached an accommodation with John Smith and continued contributing his undoubted talents to the fight for the economic policies he believed in.

Lingering disappointment over the General Election and Bryan's departure had to be put behind me, however, when I was elected to the Shadow Cabinet in July. As Shadow Health Secretary I faced the challenge of battling with my opposite number on the Government Front Bench, Virginia Bottomley, at that time the darling of the media. I relished the opportunity of getting to grips with a portfolio on which I had had strong views since my youth.

I found, however, that it is very different being in the Shadow Cabinet than being a junior frontbencher. As a member of the Shadow Cabinet, it is not permissible to put down any questions for oral answer in the House other than those which relate to one's own brief, and understandably much harsher treatment is meted out to those who are no longer merely part of a frontbench team but in charge of one.

Back in June 1987, when I had made my maiden speech, as is customary, no one had interrupted so everything had gone smoothly. My first few speeches had also passed without incident and been less daunting than I had anticipated. After a while, however, with more experience, I came to recognise that the mood in the Chamber can change swiftly and sometimes unpredictably. If misjudged, the resulting outcome can sap self-confidence. It is particularly daunting when a member is being barracked mercilessly from all sides, as sometimes happens when a speaker has lost the support of his own Party and there are mutterings of a 'poor show'. The other side then feeds on this and attacks more vigorously. If on the other hand, a speaker is on form, then the barracking can be invigorating. I relish a good fight with a worthy opponent.

It is important to remember, though, that it is impossible to perform well on every occasion and one must not worry too much if things do not go as well as hoped. There will be good speeches and bad speeches. Having suffered varying degrees of success and failure over the years, I have come to the conclusion that the ability to judge accurately the mood of the House is all-important. Equally vital is the confidence to relax sufficiently in order to rely on memory and wit rather than too heavily on written notes. A poem I wrote shortly after I entered the House of Commons tries to convey some of my thoughts about political life:

> Too much I read of that which I have
>   written
> And if not written, wished that I had.
> Too oft I hear the echo reflected
> From the wall that I myself have built
> And fail to recognise the words
> Which bounce back in my face.

For Alastair, Hugh and Andrew the question of which job I might be offered in the Shadow Cabinet took on more significance than it did for the world at large. Their concern was so great that they suggested writing a letter to John Smith, appealing to him not to make their Dad Shadow Education Secretary because he was keen on homework and discipline and would make their lives a misery. They were worried about what their teachers might say and what would be expected of them, and in fact said they would consider changing their names!

I am glad to say that I dissuaded them from taking such drastic action and, although John Smith decided to offer me the Health job, Tony Blair was to take up the challenge just over two years later. By now, my sons are resigned to my evangelical zeal for education improvement, and, happily, so is their school.

Shortly after I had taken over the job of shadowing Virginia Bottomley as Health Secretary, I had the pleasure of listening to Gillian Shephard, who was Employment Secretary, giving an after-dinner speech. We were among a number of guests at an event organised by the pharmaceutical industry. After chatting with my immediate neighbour, I examined, as I usually do, the place setting and made a general enquiry about the nature of the first course at the dinner. Having discovered a finger bowl and verified that it was not an additional soup course (always a danger), I awaited with interest to see what shellfish or other appropriate dish would arrive which warranted the use of my fingers.

I waited in vain. The first course passed without event. The main course and the pudding all went by without the necessity of using a finger bowl. By the time coffee was served, I had reluctantly arrived at the only conclusion that could be drawn.

Turning to my neighbour, I tentatively enquired, 'Do I take it that I am the only one with a finger bowl, or have all of us missed a course?'

The embarrassed and slightly awkward response confirmed my worst fears. 'Yes I'm afraid they must have thought that er . . . um . . . as you couldn't see, it would be helpful.'

'Yes,' I said and smiled to myself. When you need a finger bowl, you cannot get one, but when you don't need it, and no one else has one, they give you one.

Such is life: a juggling act between people's thoughtfulness and the clumsy implication that if you cannot see you cannot use a knife and fork either!

If truth be told, in restaurants and at dinners I tend to avoid the most awkward dishes. What I have had to catch up with — something I was not taught at school — is etiquette. It is a matter of slowing down and finding the means to avoid embarrassment such as occurs when others indicate they are watching closely your every move, as with 'Can I cut that up for you?' or 'You appear to be having some difficulty with that meat, shall I do it for you?' The point is not that such offers of help are unwelcome — quite the opposite: the more confident I become the more likely I am to actually ask someone if they would give me a hand with a particularly difficult operation such as filleting a fish or getting the meat off a bone. It is all about the way the offer is made. A quiet voice, an easy, friendly approach and one offer of help rather than several embarrassing interventions all assist in making it a perfectly natural and welcome thing to do.

Coping with meals in restaurants, however, is relatively easy when compared to coping with airline meals and three sons! For a much-needed break during the summer of 1992, I took Alastair, Hugh and Andrew to Vancouver to visit my old schoolfriend, Graeme McCreath. A better climate and a more prosperous future as a physiotherapist had lured him to settle on Vancouver Island, in the town of Victoria, following the break-up of his marriage.

It was with some trepidation that I embarked on the nine-hour flight — but we managed. No food ended up in the lap or adorned the tie and the boys were very well behaved. I have to say — and I think anyone who is being

honest would have to agree – that the strain of supervising three boys, even when staying with friends, is very
wearing. Although not insurmountable, it does add a
dimension which makes it difficult to relax, which, after
all, is what holidays should be all about. Fortunately
Graeme, his wife Christine and their three small
children have a swimming pool in their garden and
this helped enormously in keeping the boys occupied.
Vancouver has a temperate climate: the summer at its
peak is scorching hot, but cooler evenings and enough
rain in the winter keep things green and pleasant.

The part of the holiday I remember most vividly is
a trip to the McCreaths' cabin on the edge of a lake
some forty-five minutes' drive from Victoria. Graeme
and Christine had bought it as a holiday retreat. Armed
with sleeping bags and various provisions, we made an
overnight stay there.

The jetty, which Graeme assured me came with the
cabin, seemed to be shared by other neighbours, so we
were on view. Paddling the canoe, swimming from the
jetty and trying to avoid the waterskiers made for a
pleasant afternoon. It was only walking back which
caused me some aggravation. Very narrow wooden
planking linked the main jetty to the shore and, one
after the other, we crossed it, Alastair and Andrew in
front of me, and Hugh just behind. Dignity forbade me
to feel too cautiously where I was putting my feet and
Hugh's presumption that I knew what I was doing pre-
cluded him from giving me any meaningful guidance
on the dangers ahead. So it was that a moment later the
waters of the lake closed over my head as I stepped
from the plank and disappeared into the depths. When
a few seconds later I reappeared still clutching a pair of
sandals in one hand and a towel in the other, Hugh's

reaction was to ask, 'What are you doing, Dad?' It was not the first and it will not be the last time that, in a manner of speaking, I have gone in at the deep end!

On this occasion I was glad to get back to the cabin and take a shower, albeit in water which was extra-ordinary for its smell. A sulphur well supplied the cabin and at that time the necessary equipment had not been installed to remove the gases before it arrived through the taps and shower in a form which literally took your breath away.

We arrived back in England having had a most enjoyable holiday, but with me feeling more exhausted than before we set out.

My home in Sheffield, while not boasting a swimming pool, does have the enormous advantage of woodland at the bottom of the garden. The idyllic picture this conjures up has been somewhat tempered by the decision some thirty years ago to drive an urban motorway through the middle of the woods and, while not within sight of my home, it is most certainly within earshot. Nevertheless the woods are wonderful for allowing me to relax and the dog to let off steam. Following a regular and familiar route means I have few problems when the dog is running free, except when snow is on the ground and paths become more difficult to define. I have had encounters with low tree branches on a number of occasions, but these pale in significance when compared with one instance when I misjudged the bridge while crossing the stream and had to walk home covered in mud from head to toe.

One day, emerging from the woods, I called Offa. He was the best dog I have had on recall, but, on this occasion, I could discern no sign of him. He would normally come to heel and nudge my waiting hand. I shouted for what seemed a long time, coaxing in the early stages, sharpening to stern command as my desperation grew, but there was still no sign of Offa. I was about to give up and make my way home to see if he had returned there, when a passing couple enquired if I had two dogs.

'No, just one,' was my puzzled reply.

'Well, that's all right then,' they said, 'he's been sitting beside you for the past five minutes.' We all enjoyed a good laugh. He had obviously decided to see how long it would take me to realise he was there.

Offa's antics were also the cause of another amusing incident while we were walking in these woods. One day I was following quite closely behind two elderly ladies who were evidently engrossed in conversation, totally oblivious to us. Offa was playing alongside me, retrieving large sticks as he loved to do. The bigger they were, the better he liked them. Then quite suddenly the peace was broken by loud screams and shouts up ahead where an obvious skirmish was taking place. It transpired that Offa had dashed ahead of me with a four-foot-long branch in his jaws and, in his enthusiasm, had forced a path between the two ladies who barred his way, almost lifting them off their feet. We all laughed when they said they thought they were being attacked from the rear and were quite relieved to find it was only my dog. I could not help smiling to myself on the way home as I enjoyed the mental picture of Offa disappearing up the path with a passenger on each end of his branch.

But I knew our time together was drawing to a close. My heavy responsibilities, including taking on the chairmanship of the Party, meant that we were spending more time than ever travelling the country and Offa was beginning to show, in little ways, that he had had enough and was ready to retire: a reluctance to enter the House as the week progressed and a lack of enthusiasm for the harness.

It had already been agreed between the GDBA and myself shortly after Offa's stomach operation that he should retire as soon as a suitable replacement could be found and trained. While the GDBA began the search for a successor, my prime concern was to find an appropriate retirement home for him since I was not in a position to keep him myself. After a busy and varied career, Offa still needed an environment which would provide plenty of stimulation, with company and exercise in the daytime, as well as care and affection. When Paddy March, the vet in Bristol who had saved Offa's life, renewed his earlier offer that he and his family would happily foster him, the problem was resolved. Since both of them obviously liked and trusted each other, and Paddy had three children for Offa to play with, this seemed the ideal solution – and so it has proved.

The GDBA, meanwhile, was finding it harder than expected to find a replacement of the same calibre as Offa. A beautiful Golden Labrador looked promising for a while, but, as his training progressed, it became evident that he was too easily distracted. He was judged to be a potential guide dog, but not the right one for me. I was not sorry as memories of Ruby and the prospect of golden hairs clinging to trousers, carpets and furnishings made me reluctant to take on another Labrador.

Next the GDBA considered a lovely collie/golden retriever cross – a mini version of Offa. He was a delightful young dog of seventeen months and I liked him very much when we tried him out round the Houses of Parliament and in the surrounding streets. He was even introduced to John Smith in the cafeteria, but our partnership was not to be. The very next day he took off after a cat while on harness and had to be taken back to the centre for further training. I will always wonder whether Offa had a word in his ear when they were romping together in St James's Park – 'I should blot your copybook and get out of this pretty damn quick, if I were you, unless you want to suffer the House of Commons, day in, day out for the next eight years or so.'

As month after month went by and the autumn of 1993 approached, I had to break the bad news to Offa that it looked as if he would have to endure another winter in the Commons. Was he perhaps irreplaceable, we were beginning to wonder.

10

We Shall See . . .

I LOVE CYCLING and own a tandem which I keep at Clumber Park, 3,800 acres of beautiful heath and woodland within thirty minutes' drive of my home. The National Trust own the park and are kind enough to store my tandem along with the hundreds of cycles for hire. While I only manage to get out once or twice during the summer, when I do, I find it the best relaxation in the world, as well as a wonderful way to keep fit.

It was on Majorca that I first experienced the pleasure of riding a tandem. I enjoy the freedom of cycling along the lanes and byways, sometimes dawdling, sometimes at speed, the sun on my back, catching scents on the breeze. I love the salt sea spray on my lips or the waft of scorched earth, of almond and fig trees, wayside flowers and herbs as we meander down country lanes. The sound of waves on the headland, the wide open spaces of the plains and that life-giving sunshine, pushing away the memories of smoke-filled rooms and political debate, will be cherished throughout autumn and winter until spring returns once more.

The two-week holiday with my sons during the summer is about the only time throughout the year for relaxation. I cannot be reached by telephone and the

correspondence is left behind. Friends sometimes
accompany us, usually abroad to guarantee sunshine.
Pollensa in northern Majorca is a favourite spot, where
we take a wonderful villa in total isolation, approached
by a track across a cornfield, against a backdrop of the
Formentor mountains. Totally unspoilt by the brash
developments found elsewhere, it offers an ideal retreat.
Happy days.

In 1991, by way of a change, we decided to go to
Disneyworld in Florida. I wanted to take the boys while
they were still young enough to enjoy it, but I knew
in my heart that it would probably not be the kind of
environment in which I would feel easy. Nevertheless
I duly did the round of the Universal Studios, Epcot
Centre and MGM and did enjoy them. Magic Kingdom
was different though. There, more than anywhere
else, I wished I could see what was going on. I was
surrounded by so much activity and enjoyment but felt
that I was not really part of it. So much of the pleasure
is visual and I believe the disappointment I felt was borne
of frustration. I tried to encourage the boys to enjoy
themselves while they had the chance, as strangely they
needed to be pushed and cajoled into making the most
of it.

For me the happiest memory is not of Disneyworld
but Gatorland with its hundreds of sharp-toothed
inhabitants. Walking in the tranquil glades, on the
wooden suspension bridges spanning the water, close to
the bird and insect life in the heavy foliage of the trees,
was for me an experience to treasure. When the alligator show commenced, Hugh, who typically was the
first volunteer, was asked to select an alligator for the
wrestling match. When asked where he came from, he
responded, 'Sheffield, England.' Gales of laughter then

rose from the audience when the keeper retorted, 'You won't see many alligators there!' I will never forget the snap of the alligators' jaws as they leapt to catch the chickens being tossed to them. The thought of those jaws closing round its prey made me shudder.

However, politics has its own way of snapping at people's heels, as I was shortly to discover.

One major event in early February 1994 was the launch of 'Health 2000', an original consultation document which I had been working on throughout the previous year. It had fallen very much on my shoulders to draft the document which was, in effect, Labour's alternative to the Government's market-led approach to the National Health Service. This is not the place to detail the to-ing and fro-ing which occurred as the document went through the policy process during one of my busiest and least relaxing Christmas recesses in years, but eventually, with the solid and welcome support of John Smith, the document was agreed. Its successful launch that February was for me slightly overshadowed on the political stage by the unconnected controversy which followed.

At that time, debates were raging inside and outside Parliament over whether or not the age of consent for homosexuals should be lowered from twenty-one, and if so, whether it should be to eighteen or sixteen, the latter being the age of consent for heterosexuals. As Shadow Health Secretary, my postbag was always heavy but, as the lobby groups raised the temperature of argument to boiling point and coverage in the media increased, correspondence from interested parties and the general public arrived by the sackload.

I was well aware that since I am widely regarded as being part of an embattled minority because I am blind,

the pro-sixteen lobbyists would expect me to vote for
them. On the other hand, strong representations were
made to me, as to all other MPs, by those who wanted
the age of consent lowered to only eighteen, and indeed
by those who did not want it to be lowered at all.
I realised fairly early on that the easy option would be
to vote for sixteen. After carefully weighing up the
arguments of all three factions, however, I followed my
conscience and voted for eighteen.

There were a number of reasons for this decision but
chief among them is the belief that eighteen is the
appropriate age of consent for heterosexuals and homosexuals alike. Since this is not the appropriate place to
examine the issues or my reasons in detail, suffice it
to say that, while some may regard me as old-fashioned,
I can categorically state that I am not in any way
homophobic. I hold strong views about the need for all
of us to develop a society in which care and respect for
others are fostered and acted upon. In order for people
to understand the sharing and fulfilment which come
from a loving relationship, it is essential that they should
not treat sexual intercourse as casually as blowing their
nose.

Allowing young people time to grow up does not
seem to me to be a particularly reactionary concept,
although I do fully accept that the provision of
maximum advice and information is essential. In this
regard I take a completely contrary view to the moralists
on the Far Right of the political spectrum, something
which those on the Left find difficult to conceive. All
my life I have refused to believe in the black and white
lines drawn by those who expect everyone who agrees
on one subject or area of policy to concur automatically
on others. In general I am Left wing and radical on

economic policy but conservative on social matters. This is the very reverse of the attitudes and actions of the Labour Party throughout the eighties and early nineties, when the Party itself was out of tune with the electorate in general.

Offa, however, was blissfully unaware of all this controversy; he may have noticed an increase in the crowds of protesters we had to negotiate in the central lobby and outside Parliament, but as an old hand he took it in his stride. For me the real test was yet to come: both in the events which occurred in the months immediately following, with the untimely death of John Smith, and in the undoubted drop in my popularity because of the age of consent vote which I knew would affect both the Shadow Cabinet and National Executive elections the following autumn.

Even after eight years, I am still not entirely comfortable in the cocoon-like atmosphere of the House of Commons. This slight feeling of alienation on my part has been increased by the difficulty in socialising and relating to other MPs; it is a considerable disadvantage not being able to spot them in the corridor or tea room. It is widely assumed that everyone takes account of my blindness and will come over to speak to me but this is by no means always the case. I know I must still work harder to maintain contact with colleagues and find opportunities to talk to them. The need to do so is particularly acute when in Opposition in the sense that, if we were in government and I were fortunate enough to be in the Cabinet, I would be judged by how well I was running a department and on my ability to win over the electorate to support the policies being implemented, whereas in Opposition informal contact with fellow Members is much more important.

There is no such thing as a normal day in my life as an MP. The only regular routine is rising early – I tend to wake earlier as the years go by – and getting to bed too late. Whether on Monday mornings in Sheffield or for the remainder of the week in London, my domestic arrangements are much like anyone else's. 'Mashing' a cup of tea, as we say in Yorkshire, eating my muesli and feeding the dog are all part of the regular pattern. Encouraging the dog to 'spend a penny' is an essential first step of the morning, followed by regular grooming which indicates to the dog the imminent buckling on of the harness. When in London, our daily trek down to the local underground station, which is about ten minutes' walk away, is as near as we get to fresh air and exercise. We pass near to the Wimbledon All England Tennis Club, where in 1989 I had the good fortune to watch the Chris Evert and Steffi Graf semi-final. I was captivated by the atmosphere and my poem attempts to express what I felt about this eccentric, but quite quintessentially English, fortnight each summer.

> Centre Court, cocooned
> Warm and comfortable
> Untouched by accents
> Alien to our own.
> People who think
> They own all about them.
> Enjoying the sunshine
> Melting in the heat.
> Togetherness
> Borne of easy friendship
> And shared experience.
>
> The ancient grounds
> Green and spacious

The scent of strawberries and hay
Grass roasting in midday sun.
Centre Court, tension,
Click of ball on racquet
The echo, the call of umpire
'Quiet please'
We're thinking.

When I first entered the Commons, I was given a very small room, albeit to myself, on one of the upper corridors, close to where the main committee rooms are situated. At the time of writing, I have a much larger and more comfortable room just off Speaker's Court, adjoining the Speaker's House and facilities. This is situated directly below Tony Blair's office as Leader of the Opposition and gives access on to New Palace Yard. It is possible to exercise the dog on the lawn which adjoins the fountain and, since very few people venture there, there is no danger of upsetting anyone.

There was a journalist on an evening paper who tried to make a story out of nothing by suggesting that other MPs had complained about my earlier dog, Teddy, doing a whoopsie on the grass in New Palace Yard. I called his bluff and said I would comment on the story if he could identify for me who had complained. I heard nothing further. Offa too was falsely accused, not only by the tabloids but also by supposedly responsible broadsheets such as the *Guardian* and the *Sunday Telegraph*, of biting people in the Palace of Westminster and even of lifting his leg on a statue in the Central Lobby. All this was, of course, pure fabrication. No trained guide dog would ever behave in such a way, although that does not mean they cannot be mischievous.

One of the frustrations of the House of Commons is

the belief, fostered by some newspapers, that MPs are not working unless they are in the Chamber. The truth is the very opposite. Sitting on benches, forming an audience, is an essential part of the working of parliamentary democracy but it is not the hard graft. It can, in fact, sometimes be a very welcome break in an otherwise very busy round of speech-making, meetings, drafting of policy and of course visits to schools and colleges. Listening is a highly important aspect of an MP's role. Pressure groups, experts, representatives of every part of the education service not only expect to be heard but feel aggrieved if it is not possible for either myself or a member of the Education Team to be able to meet and talk with them.

The resources available to MPs and to the Opposition front bench are extremely limited compared with those in other developed democracies. Shadow Cabinet members receive just about adequate funding to run an office. All those working for MPs in their constituency or in the Commons tend to work uncertain hours. Working evenings and weekends is not uncommon in order to ensure that I am brought up to date with urgent material. The additional task of getting material brailled or on to tape adds yet another chore to an often unsung job.

The secretarial work is undertaken by Sarah Young and Alison Bartlett in my London office and by Valda and Jean in Sheffield. Sophie Linden and Anne Pinney undertake the research side of the job, gathering information I need, and reading on to tape items from the daily newspapers, background material and reports. I then listen to the tapes over a coffee or sandwich at lunchtime and late into the evening when I also deal with the endless flow of correspondence, which increases as government actions raise concerns and my own speeches evoke a reaction.

Conor Ryan took over from Mike Lee shortly after I became Shadow Health Secretary and uses his longstanding skills with the press and broadcast media to promote what we are doing and to try to damp down the misinterpretation which regrettably is a continuing feature of British political reporting. In modern terms, I suppose he might be described as a spin doctor.

As winter gave way to spring in 1994, the political focus shifted to canvassing for the forthcoming Local and European Elections in which, as Chairman of the Party, I was bound to take a leading role. In light of the pressure of commitments, I had agreed with the GDBA that, when Offa's replacement was eventually chosen, the new dog and I would undergo training on a peripatetic basis. Instead of spending the usual three weeks together at a residential training centre, followed by several weeks' supervision, we would spend about four days at home getting to know each other and working through any major problems, followed by training while I went about my normal business, under the direction of a supervisor. The idea was to make it easier for me to fulfil my commitments, although it was bound to be more demanding for the dog.

I knew that Offa was ready for retirement. I, too, was eager for the matter to be resolved although I did not look forward to parting with him. At last, one day in late March, word came through that Offa's successor had passed all the tests thus far and it was time for her to pay a visit to Westminster.

Lucy, a shining black curly-coated retriever/Labrador cross of eighteen months, turned out to be a delightful smaller version of Teddy. As a test run, her informal introduction to the House of Commons could hardly have been more auspicious. I sneaked her into the Chamber behind the Speaker's Chair, where we settled ourselves in the nearest available space on the front bench rather than in my usual place. I could feel her head turning from side to side as she took in everything around her. There was a great deal of noise and commotion in the House that day as it was Prime Minister's Questions, but she eventually settled down contentedly. Scarcely had she done so, however, when a furore erupted as Tory MP Tony Marlow called upon John Major to resign over a row concerning voting percentages in the expanded European Union. There was pandemonium throughout the Chamber as MPs of every persuasion shouted, booed, clapped and waved order papers. I kept my hand on Lucy's head to reassure her and check she was not in any distress, but she remained oblivious to the mayhem around us.

When we left the Chamber to rejoin Peter Smith, her trainer, we took Lucy for a welcome walk round Parliament Square. Here the heavy traffic pollution caused her to have a sneezing fit and we had to dissuade her from seeking sanctuary in the more salubrious air of Westminster Abbey. When the time came for Peter to take her back to the training centre, it was felt that Lucy had made a most creditable debut on her first stint in Westminster and her future career in politics was assured.

Over the following few weeks, campaigning for local and European elections shifted into top gear with a heavy schedule of speaking engagements round the country, as well as my usual commitments. In the midst of the campaigning and the tensions inherent in the

imminent change-over of dogs, came the news of John
Smith's tragic death on 12 May.

Although I knew John and his wife Elizabeth
before he took over leadership of the Labour Party, our
collaboration following my appointment as Party
Chairman had inevitably drawn us closer. On the night
before his death, I had the pleasure of being seated next
to Elizabeth at a special fundraising dinner in London,
at which John made an excellent and largely unscripted
speech. The last I saw of John was when he and
Elizabeth left for a drink with the then leader of the
French Socialists, Michel Rocard, before going back to
their flat in the Barbican.

News of John's sudden death was a devastating
personal blow as well as a political one. As is widely
known, he had suffered a heart attack five years earlier
but had confided solely in Elizabeth when, a week
before his death, he experienced chest pains during
and after the ceremony marking the official opening
of the Channel Tunnel by the Queen and President
Mitterrand. John had kept going in the best interests of
the Party, knowing that in the middle of an election
campaign, taking a rest would have given rise to
speculation about his health. On the day of his death,
when I said he had given his life for the Labour Party,
I meant precisely that.

A few months before John Smith's death, he had
invited Shadow Cabinet members and other close
colleagues to the flat Elizabeth and he had just taken
over on the thirty-third floor of the tower block at
the Barbican. It was a spacious flat and we were made
warmly welcome.

On occasions of this sort, I try to build a picture not
only of those present but also of the surroundings.

I asked various colleagues to describe what they could see across the city from such a vantage point. Their comments and my own feelings of soaring in the lift as floor after floor swept by I combined into a poem which I was never able to show John, but which I feel sure Elizabeth would understand. In the same way that for me Sheffield is home, so Edinburgh was John and Elizabeth's home and London merely a place of work. I would therefore like to dedicate this poem to Elizabeth Smith, now Baroness Smith of Gilmore Hill.

A Visit to the Barbican

Challenger Three, I thought,
As the lift soared
Ten, fifteen, twenty, thirty, thirty-five floors.

Doors open on to a landing,
Still, eerie, silent.
Then, from a door beyond,
The sound of voices.
People, laughing,
Conversing about little or nothing,
Here in the sky.

Is this, I ask myself,
A vision of the future?
Capsules circling the earth,
Distant from human life
Freed from London's traffic din,
But freed too from reality on the ground.

For thirty-five floors high
In the Cromwell Tower,
No birds are heard to sing,
No leaves to scatter in the wind.

Views are wondrous, yes,
But like gazing down
On a Lilliput of life.

Here you meet no one,
And no one meets you.
Alone in the sky
On the thirty-fifth floor
You could disappear from the world
And never be noticed,
Until, your bills unpaid,
Reveal you to have gone
Into orbit forever.

Lost to the world of men
And the love of womankind.

For Labour, the forthcoming elections were an essential test of electoral strength and, as a lifelong avid pro-European, John's memory could best be commemorated by success at the polls. The next ten days were very stressful as I discussed with colleagues the most effective means of restoring stability to the election campaign and to the selection of a successor to John. In addition to this, the time had come to say farewell to Offa.

Amid all this turmoil, it might have been sensible to postpone Lucy's starting date for working with me, but Peter Smith was due to go to the United States and I wanted to get the transfer completed before the end of the parliamentary session. It was therefore adjudged, correctly as it transpired, that training with Lucy on the job in both Sheffield and London as well as around the country as part of the election campaign, rather than training with her in a totally different artificial environment, would be an excellent means of introducing

her to the real world of my work. Thus it was decided
that Offa should be retired on 25 May and that Peter
and Lucy would join me on the election trail.

On Monday 23 May, there were numerous photo-
calls for the media who wanted farewell shots of Offa.
Photographers pressed for me to pose sitting beside
him with my arm around his shoulder, and while I may
have appeared to be in control, I was fighting to keep
back the tears as I said farewell to my faithful friend.
Offa remained stoical while I struggled to appear so.

Two days later, when the time came to hand Offa
over to Peter Smith, I gave him a farewell hug and
tickled his ears. He went off happily, as if he were
simply departing to spend another short holiday at the
Guide Dog Centre as he had so many times before. He
could not know that this time it was for ever and that
we would never see each other again. As the door of
my office closed behind them, I just stood silently in
the middle of the room for several minutes feeling
quite bereft. No matter that Offa would enjoy his new
life and home, I felt his loss acutely at that moment and
for a long time to come.

On Friday 27 May, Lucy began her official duties. I
knew from the start that she was going to be a very
lively companion as I had received advance warning
from Mrs Smith, her puppy walker in Preston, who
had written to me with some amusing anecdotes about
the time Lucy spent with them:

Lucy was my second puppy-walking assignment.
My supervisor suggested that I might like to try
'something more challenging' than my previous
dog. One glance at Lucy at the Bolton training
centre proved what an evil sense of humour she
has. She was much taller than the two Labrador

puppies that were with her, with uncontrollable legs and ears. She was busily organising the bewildered pups in a game of leaf chase, and convinced herself that the pup cowering in the corner loved being dragged by the ears to join the game. I stood in silence with my eldest son and several other puppy walkers until someone mentioned that Lucy looked 'something of a live wire'.

At first she did not welcome the suggestion that she might become a guide dog one day. She felt her real forte was operatic singing and she practised her scales every night for five weeks. Then she found a new career in furniture design with a special penchant for three-legged chairs. My sons thought she was brilliant and called her 'the naughtiest puppy ever'. We used to introduce her as 'Lucy, short for Lucifer'.

She was such a characterful puppy that when she was going back to Bolton for training, I remarked to my supervisor that she would need a lot of brain activity to keep her out of mischief and she should preferably go to someone with a sense of humour!

But please beware of muddy ditches. I hope you have not discovered her enthusiasm for hurtling through them, nose down, throwing the water over her head . . .

When Lucy arrived at my home in Sheffield, she explored every nook and cranny of her new garden, bouncing around on her long, springy legs. Within a very short time the lawn was littered with sticks which she had retrieved from the hedge and tossed into the air in her enjoyment. Yet the moment the harness was put on, she would become calm and mature, recognising that she had a job to do. Lucy and I took to each other immediately. During our first weekend together, we concentrated on attempting to achieve in four days what would normally require three weeks in a training centre. She appeared relaxed with family and friends, and generally assumed her new role with amazing ease.

On a short walk round the neighbourhood she behaved so well that we decided to take her into the city centre to introduce her to Valda and Jean in my office and to test her in the busy streets. Lucy's performance was outstanding and I could discern Peter's pleasure from the smile in his voice. He confirmed that he was delighted with her – we both were. The major test, however, was yet to come. Peter kept a close watch as we headed back to London. Despite the House being in recess, we had a hectic schedule of meetings, speeches and press conferences as well as further campaigning visits around the country. In addition, Lucy made her debut on BBC Television's *Question Time*.

There was no time to break Lucy in gently, however, as the tempo of work increased. In addition to the Local and European Elections taking place on 9 June, the leadership contest was beginning to gather momentum. Since John's death, all my endeavours, as Chairman, had been focused on how I could quickly draw together everyone within the Party in order to prevent its disintegration, and to maximise the benefits of unity, which were John's legacy. Margaret Beckett, the Acting Leader, and I worked in tandem to ensure that we had a clear perspective on the plans we formulated and that we put these across succinctly and firmly to all sections of the Party, particularly to potential candidates for the leadership.

It rapidly became clear, however, that there was to be

a complication in that Margaret herself was being encouraged to stand for the leadership. Had she remained Deputy Leader, there would have been no challenge to her position, but once her decision was made to stand for the leadership, then it meant that both positions were up for grabs. Robin Cook and Gordon Brown both felt that their chances were slim and had decided to resist the considerable public pressure brought to bear upon them to stand for the leadership. The three candidates were therefore to be Margaret Beckett, Tony Blair and John Prescott.

Over the following weeks my purpose was to remain neutral and ensure that the timetable which the General Secretary of the Party and I had put to the National Executive Committee was carried out. It became apparent early on that Tony Blair would win a resounding victory, but the contest continued with dignity through to election day and the launch of the new leader from the foundation which John Smith had built.

Just before the election of the new leader I wrote in the *Daily Mirror* how Tony Blair and I shared a belief in the values of community and a clear identity of purpose on social policy. I looked forward to working with him in the years ahead in the development of those ideas, but of course I did not know at the time exactly what role I was to play.

At that stage French socialists were in retreat following devastating parliamentary elections, the SPD in Germany seemed unlikely to win the October election (and they did not), and in the USA the Democrats were struggling in the run-up to the congressional elections. Tony Blair acknowledged clearly that now was the time for the Labour Party to take a very positive lead. He recognised that complacency was still a danger and that, despite opinion poll leads, we had a mountain to climb to keep the electorate with us through to the General Election.

Meanwhile I wondered what the political future might hold in store for me. If the incident which had occurred when Lucy and I made our first official appearance together on the floor of the House of Commons was anything to go by, then the auguries for the future were favourable. Despite having entered the Chamber several times with Lucy to accustom her to the Labour front bench, when the day came for our first formal appearance together, she made her own decision. Labour's recent success in the European elections had led her to believe that we had taken over government and she thought a brisk walk to the Government despatch box was called for. Helpful Labour colleagues hastily came to our rescue and at the last minute redirected us to the Labour front bench. Afterwards when people remarked that Lucy had taken me to the wrong side of the Chamber, I replied that she had in fact taken me to the right side, but a couple of years too soon!

Following the Labour Party Conference in October 1994 and the Shadow Cabinet elections shortly afterwards, I was appointed Shadow Education Secretary, a post which I relished taking on, given that I have always held strong views on the subject. I am enjoying working with my new Education team of Bryan Davies, Peter Kilfoyle and Estelle Morris, and I look forward to meeting the continuing challenges ahead. In the meantime, Lucy and I will certainly be busy; doubtless the usual quota of crises and controversies will come our way.

Politics is a fickle world and we politicians are judged by the events of the moment, sometimes even by the last speech we have delivered. As a friend recently observed, quoting an aphorism of Goethe's, 'As a general rule the most significant period in the life of an individual is that of his development. Later we have his conflict with the world, and that is interesting only in so far as it produces results.'

We shall see . . .

PHOTOGRAPH ACKNOWLEDGEMENTS

INDEX